A FAMILY AT WAR

THE TALBOTS OF LITTLE GADDESDEN

Roger and Julia Bolton

Grosvenor House
Publishing Limited

This book is published by
Grosvenor House Publishing Ltd
28-30 High Street, Guildford, Surrey, GU1 3EL.
www.grosvenorhousepublishing.co.uk

A CIP record for this book
is available from the British Library

ISBN 978-1-78148-636-8

To Andrew Graham-Stewart and to Dawn Webster
of Kiplin Hall who kept the letters.

Contents

Introduction

In 2011, twenty years after we moved into the main part of The Manor House in Little Gaddesden, a package arrived in the post from Andrew Graham Stewart who had sold us the property. He was about to move homes in Scotland and was clearing out some old papers. Among them were letters and documents belonging to Kathleen Talbot who had lived in the Manor House from the early 1920's until her death in 1958. The house had passed to her friend and companion Dorothy Erhart and then to Andrew's father, who had eventually divided it between his four sons. Kathleen was childless and had never married, nor had her elder sister Bridget, or her two brothers Humphrey and Geoffrey. The Talbots of Little Gaddesden had died out.

Once a dominant family in the area, allied to the Brownlows of Ashridge, who had also died childless, all these Talbots had left behind in the village were some of their tombstones in the churchyard and the two houses in which they had lived, Little Gaddesden House, the family home, and The Manor House, to which Kathleen moved after the First World War, a war which had destroyed their world. As the last Graham-Stewart brother to leave the Manor House complex, Andrew had felt a responsibility to preserve the papers. Now after twenty years he felt that they could be safely returned to Kathleen's former home.

We felt a strange sensation sifting the documents and reading them, as if we were invading someone's privacy, though the last of the family, Bridget Talbot, had died forty years before.

The package consisted of a book of poems written by a local vicar who appeared to be in love, platonically, with Kathleen's mother, Emily Louisa Augusta de Grey, and Emily's Coutts bankbooks. There was a copy of the will of an aunt, the wife of a Victorian war hero, General Sir Reginald Talbot, and a 17th century prayer book from the now destroyed Bridgewater House in London, which must have come from Ashridge where the Earls of Bridgewater had lived before the Brownlows.

There were various receipts which showed that K (as Kathleen was always known) had owned property in London and travelled post war to Java and Australia, and a guest book with the signatures of some who had visited her at The Manor House. Finally there were the letters, some from prisoner of war camps in Germany in 1917, some from her brothers and sister, the vast majority from the First World War years. They were difficult to read, particular those from Bridget, but they showed four children trying to hold a family and a way of life together, in times of utmost stress. Searching the internet we discovered that there were more Talbot letters in existence. Sometime in the early 1980s, when Bridget's former home, Little Gaddesden House, was being altered, some old papers had been thrown onto a skip, from which, thankfully, they had been retrieved. They are now at Kiplin Hall in North Yorkshire, Bridget's second home, which she had been given by a cousin and which she had helped save from destruction. We drove up to Kiplin where the curator, Dawn Webster, showed us round the beautiful 17th century property, now run by a trust, which has photos and diaries of the Talbots, together with some paintings and engravings. We have now deposited 'our' Talbot letters at Kiplin Hall, where they are in the safest of hands. Before doing so, however, we transcribed them, and this little book is an edited collection of those letters, interspersed with biography, part of Bridget's diary, and some 'Kiplin' letters. It tells the story of a lost family and a lost time.

We hope that you will enjoy it, that Kathleen and Bridget, and Humphrey and Geoffrey, will forgive our invasion of their privacy, and that their parents, Emily and Alfred, will admire the way that their children coped with adversity, (with a little help from Fortnum and Mason).

We certainly do.

Roger and Julia Bolton,
The Manor House,
Little Gaddesden,
Hertfordshire

2013

Chapter 1

Before the War

Dear K,
You don't deserve any letters as you haven't answered mine.
However as I have found a nice piece of cotton grass I am sending
it to you and if you don't care for it you can give it to Angel.

K was ten year old Kathleen Talbot who lived in Little Gaddesden
House. Angel was K's friend, the daughter of the Ashridge
Agent Colonel Wheatley and the writer was twenty year old
Humphrey Talbot.
(K kept the grass all her life and it lies before us as we write)
It was September 1904 and her elder brother, called H or Old
Ginger, was holidaying with his nineteen year old sister, Bridget in
Glen Canisp, Loch Inver, Lairg in North Britain (*The address was
printed on the paper, presumably by an Englishman*). H seemed to
be having a good old time:-

Bridget and I made an expedition to the top of Canisp this
afternoon. Uncle Addy fished in loch NaGainimh but did not
catch anything. It was very jolly on the top of the mountain but
rather cold and windy. We both put stones on the cairn and
I found a horseshoe which had come off a horse which, with
some others, escaped from a camp of Lovat's scouts about two
months *(ago)* and ran away right to the top of Canisp. They were
trying to find their way back to Uist which is one of the Hebrides
(here consult your atlas) and I suppose they thought if they went
up high they could see which way to go.

Humphrey had been stalking, but 'the rifle cartridge missed fire
just as I was going to kill a lovely stag'. Lucky stag; doubtless
it was Uncle Addy who was paying for the holiday. Addy was

1

Adelbert Wellington Brownlow Cust, 4th Baron and 3rd Earl Brownlow, who owned Belton House in Lincolnshire, Ashridge Park next to Little Gaddesden in Hertfordshire, and a fine townhouse at 8, Carlton House Terrace, off St James Park in London, a short saunter from the Athenaeum, the Reform and the other clubs of Pall Mall. He was just one of many aristocratic relatives of the Talbot children. Indeed in that year, 1904, Bridget's scrapbook records visits to the country homes of families and friends which took her away from home for a third of the year. Doubtless she was expected to become engaged to one of the eligible young men she would meet.

The children had earls and countesses for grandparents, aunts and uncles. Their Talbot grandfather, the 18th Earl of Shrewsbury, was one of eleven children, nine of whom married and had children. Bridget's father, Alfred Talbot, had thirty six first cousins and there were many more relatives on both his and their mother's side. One of Alfred's brothers, Walter, later an Admiral in the Royal Navy, was obliged to change his surname to Carpenter in order to inherit some property, Kiplin Hall in North Yorkshire, and had to promise to remain a Protestant. These two Talbot brothers married two sisters, Beatrice and Emily de Grey, daughters of Lord Walsingham, and the families frequently holidayed together at Kiplin.

When Alfred's sister, Adelaide, had married Earl Brownlow, several Talbots, including Alfred, had moved down from Ingestre in Staffordshire, close to the Shrewsbury ancestral home at Alton Towers, and taken country houses in the Ashridge area.

Alfred had moved into Little Gaddesden House, originally built for the now retired Ashridge Agent, William Paxton, a brother of the famous Victorian gardener and designer of the Crystal Palace, Joseph Paxton. It had lain empty since the wife of the present Agent, Colonel Wheatley, had decided she and her family should live in the nearby 16th century Manor House instead. Alfred and his wife Emily also had a fashionable London residence, 28 Cadogan Gardens, off Sloane St in Chelsea, where, in 1911, they appear to have had fifteen servants. The Talbot children often stayed in Carlton House Terrace with the Brownlows, who had no children of their own, at their Belton home in Lincolnshire, and were invited to almost every social event that took place at nearby Ashridge.

Also childless was another of Alfred's brothers, Major General the Hon. Sir Reginald Talbot CB, the 'very model of a modern Major General', a hero of the Zulu war and the Nile Expedition to rescue General Gordon. It narrowly failed, and Reggie had almost been killed.

He and his wife, the former Margaret Stuart Wortley, always called Aunt Doobit, were regarded as a model couple and were much loved and very hospitable. They lived in Manchester Square in London and later in Regent's Park Terrace. However Margaret harboured a guilty secret which was only revealed some eighty years later. While her husband was Military Attaché to Paris between 1889 and 1894 she had fallen, like an amazing number of respectable Victorian women, for the considerable physical charms of Wilfred Scawen Blunt, poet, revolutionary and life long seducer. *(His sister had been the first wife of the Ashridge Agent Colonel Wheatley, but she had died young of tuberculosis, shortly after giving birth to a son.)*

Blunt's usual tactic was to entice his quarry to Egypt, encourage them to wear free flowing Arab clothes and then take them out to lie on the sand and look at the stars. Even the patron of the poet WB Yeats, the intensely serious and moral Lady Augusta Gregory, lay down in the sand with him.

Fortunately for her and for Margaret Talbot, no children resulted from their relationships. There were Blunt offspring in many respectable country mansions. Margaret Talbot felt intensely guilty about her Parisian affair, and confessed all to her devoted husband who forgave her. Blunt then wrote a passionate love poem about her, sent it to Margaret, and she succumbed again, resulting in more guilt. Finally Margaret gave Blunt up. She was, he said, scared of the scandal which would result if their relationship became known. 'The hideous scandals involving Harry Cust', he wrote in his diary when she started to repel his advances, 'have frightened her, as they have many others, so that Harry, if not virtuous himself, is the cause of virtue in others'.

What were Harry Cust's 'hideous scandals'? The heir to Lord Brownlow had crossed a line. It was acceptable for Cust to sleep with married women of his own class, or unmarried girls of a lower class, but the seduction of a baronet's unmarried daughter was intolerable. Whether Sir Reginald knew of his wife's renewed affair with Blunt is not clear. By the early 20th century however, these Talbots appeared very happy together, perhaps because Blunt was elsewhere, pursuing fresh conquests, and their young nephews and nieces loved staying with them.

Margaret Talbot had been desperate to have children of her own, but she was childless like her sisters-in-law Gertie Pembroke and Adelaide Brownlow. Once scolded for the vanity of her ways, she replied 'because I have no children I see other women of my age with children growing up and happy through them. But what have I got in my future? They tell me I have everything I want in life and it is true, all but this one thing. How gladly I would give up beauty and pleasure and social success all for one squalling baby to keep me awake at night'.
(Margaret Talbot's secret remained safe until Blunt's diaries were published some eighty years later.)

Alfred Chetwynd-Talbot of Little Gaddesden, though having an Admiral and a General for brothers, does not seem to have had martial qualities. He was however tall and very distinguished in appearance with a high forehead. *(He appears to have gradually dropped the 'Chetwynd' from his name and his children never used it.)*
Alfred's sister Adelaide, Countess Brownlow, nee Talbot, was considered a great beauty, and she certainly looks one in a large painting of her, by Frederick, Lord Leighton, which hangs over the staircase at Belton. There is another famous Victorian painting of Adelaide, this time by G F Watts. It shows her with her two sisters, Constance, who married the 8th Marquess of Lowthian of Blickling Hall, and Gertrude, who married the 13th Earl of Pembroke and lived at Wilton.
It is difficult to be sure how independently wealthy the Talbots of Little Gaddesden were, but in terms of wealthy and aristocratic

relations they were immensely rich and it is hard, reading about those pre First World War years, not to think their offspring had a golden childhood. Alfred does not appear ever to have had a full time job and in the census is described as being of 'Private Means'. However he was a lay reader in the Church of England and he and his wife, like his sister the Countess, do seem to have had a social conscience, which some of their children inherited. The Alfred Talbots set up the local Ladies' Sewing Guild to make useful clothes which were then distributed in the village. In the particularly long and severe winter of 1891 they organised a soup kitchen three times a week at nearby Ivinghoe and Edlesborough, and they distributed sacks of coal to the tenants. Alfred also sometimes took church services at Edlesborough and was said to be the favourite brother of the Countess. His family was certainly in and out of Ashridge on an almost daily basis and the childless Brownlows seem to have been very close to their nephews and nieces.

A short biography of Alfred Chetwynd-Talbot M.A., of Wellington College and Christ Church Oxford, appears in a book called 'Hertfordshire Leaders', published in the early 20th century and intended for the subjects, their families and friends, and thus entirely positive. It states that 'he has been one of the County's most active and influential citizens since (*taking up residence*). He entertains largely, and he and his wife are, as host and hostess, two of the most popular personages in the countryside of English social life'. The writer is keen to point out of Alfred that 'although a reformer he is not a radical. He is Conservative in politics, but has never sought political office. In private life he is very fond of all out-door sports and is an enthusiastic bicyclist'. And he does have a sense of social responsibility, the writer adds. 'Perhaps his best and most conspicuous services have been rendered as a Director of the Metropolitan Association for Improving the Dwellings of the Industrial Classes'.

From 1895 to 1909, the younger members of the Talbot family produced the remarkable Cadogaddesden Gazette-presumably named after their Hertfordshire and London homes. Adults and children contributed articles, poems, drawings, watercolours, quizzes and competitions, which were collated and circulated to members.

Uncle Addy, Lord Brownlow, contributed this poem:-

If scientists would fain discuss
Such all important things
As Why the sea is boiling hot
And whether pigs have wings
In future they need only read
The Cadogaddesden's pages.
Humphrey will take Historic notes
And Geoffrey that of Sport
Bridget here will write on chess
And 'Movements of the Court'
The poorest purse may pay for it
And yet have nought to fear
The charge is nothing by the week
And twice that by the year.

Bridget (14) Geoffrey (11) and Humphrey (15) were the Editors when the Easter 1899 issue came out.
Presumably K (5) was too young at that stage to contribute.

The Brownlows kept open house at Ashridge. Kings, Queens, Shahs and Indian princes passed through its doors. Lord Brownlow had served in three Conservative administrations and maintained his political connections across the parties, inviting leading politicians like Gladstone down for the weekend. The Grand Old Man read Dante to a house party after dinner, and soldiers such as K of K, Lord Kitchener of Khartoum, who had fought with Reggie Talbot in the Sudan, also took the train to Berkhamsted and made the three mile journey past the castle and through the glorious Chiltern beech woods to the massive early 19th century house, built upon the ruins of a 13th century monastery. Where monarchs like Edward 1st and Queen Elizabeth once rode, the Brownlows drove their guests in liveried coaches.

The Brownlows were also on the fringes of the 'Souls', a group of high minded, idealistic and intellectual aristocrats, whose inner circle included George Curzon, that 'most superior person' who became Viceroy of India and then Foreign Secretary, and who considered himself a failure because he didn't become Prime Minister. His rival, Arthur Balfour, who did, was also a member, as was Margot Tennant, who married another Prime Minister, Henry Asquith, and Lord Brownlow's cousin and heir, that compulsive womaniser Harry Cust. The group is said to have been named at a dinner party given by the Brownlows in 1888, when a relative, Admiral Lord Charles Beresford, mocked their intentions. 'You all sit and talk about each other's souls — I shall call you the Souls'.

Harry Cust, however, as we have seen, preferred the sensual to the spiritual. One of his friends, Evan Charteris, then a struggling young barrister, invited Harry Cust to dinner, together with an eminent solicitor he was trying to impress. Cust drank rather too much, and the next day Charteris sent him a telegram saying, 'You have ruined my life but it was worth it'.

Harry replied with another. 'That is a sentiment I am more used to hearing from women'.

If all this dazzling company was not enough to impress the young Talbot children then there was always Mrs. Humphrey Ward. The famous Victorian novelist lived three miles away in Stocks on the edge of Aldbury and frequently drove over to Ashridge with friends who were staying with her, such as the novelists Henry James and H G Wells, and the playwright Oscar Wilde, before of course he saw the inside of Reading gaol.

We can catch a glimpse of those pre Great War years at Ashridge in the diaries of Constance Sitwell, nee Talbot, and in the book, 'The Three Rectories', by her friend Constance Lane, yet another cousin. There seem to have been so many cousins called Constance or Humphrey that it is no wonder that some were often better known by their nicknames. Constance *(Cooie)* Lane said 'Ashridge had the tradition of a great house with open doors and a generous culture of hospitality. Lord and Lady Brownlow together gave it an individual charm, a fragrance, a childlike quality. Her eagerness and love of goodness, combining with his happy nature, added something unusual to their tradition of English landowners and aristocrats. If she had enthusiasm but little method, he on the contrary was neat-handed and orderly, but he lacked drive, as is often the case of sons with energetic mothers. He turned away from politics, great schemes, attending just enough to his own estates, to arranging houses and gardens to his own taste, in London attending to the House of Lords and in the country, shooting and entertaining his friends. He had the gift of enjoying things and making them interesting to other people'.

Constance Lane also described Christmas at the Alfred Talbots' home:-

The porch door of Little Gaddesden House had fairy lights round it and the door was opened by the old butler with side whiskers. The long passage with its painted walls and inlaid furniture, its giant chrysanthemums and evergreen wreaths, looked grand and partified. Round the tree, when we entered the dining room, were familiar faces, all smiling. Most of the men were tall, our host Alfred Talbot handsome and benign with a little grey beard; he always wore spats and a buttonhole, violets or a white carnation. Cousin Emily, the hostess, moved about bouncingly among the guests, hospitable and gay, attired in an Elizabethan fashion in a dark dress with slashed sleeves and jewels. The Brownlows would be there revolving among the lesser fry. A strong smell of burning fir branches mixed with the flower scents, and the flickering light of the candles with the shining of silver ribbons and brighties on the tree. We children wandered about and peeped at the parcels, neatly wrapped up and tied with ribbon, round the shining tree, while the elders greeted each other and talked in the grown-up way over our heads.... I never know which I enjoyed most, the hum of conversation round the tree, a tea time with the cousins, or driving down the drive with the fairy lights on either side of it, we children well muffled up and sitting on the back seat of the pony carriage, the carriage lamps flashing on each tree trunk along the road.

Constance *(Conty)* Talbot, later Sitwell, was born in Ceylon in 1887. Ten years later her family returned to England and lived initially in Harpenden, before moving to Marchmont House in Piccotts End, Hemel Hempstead.

She was soon visiting her Talbot cousins some five miles away and she too was fond of the chatelaine of Ashridge.

'Lady Brownlow, our beloved cousin Adelaide, once seen was never forgotten, with her proud beauty, her selflessness, and her deep and tender goodness'. She also referred to Alfred Talbot 'with his usual goodness'.

She did not however feel the same way about Alfred's younger son Geoffrey Talbot who, despite her continual rebuffs, would not stop pursuing her. Indeed, it seems as if Conty was pursued by half the neighbourhood, including Mrs. Humphrey Ward's son. Judging from her diaries, and a later portrait of her, it is easy to see why Hertfordshire's young men would be dazzled by this child of India, who later wrote books about the sub continent and headed a spiritualist movement. In her book 'Frolic Youth', she describes how Geoffrey, like his elder brother Humphrey, had gone out to India to work for the State Railway. On his leave he had chased her relentlessly. It wasn't the first time. As early as 1905, when they were both seventeen, she talks of being pursued by him. At a ball at the Rothschild's house at nearby Tring he angrily took her aside and said, according to Conty, 'Do you know why I came here? To see you! Only that really – I don't care a bit for anyone else. It was only for you, and then you chucked me. Why did you chuck me for Basil?'

Five years later, in 1910, Conty went to a dance at the Alfred Talbots' in Cadogan Gardens, perhaps to celebrate Geoffrey's return from India. The following day she said the Talbots 'had not even begun breakfast at 12.15. They giggled incessantly, thinking Geoffrey the last word in wit'. Conty clearly did not.

There were often picnics in the woods at Ashridge, and both Cooie and Conty were frequently present. Cooie Lane wrote, 'We had picnics at the tea house, a rough wooden chalet in the woods, to enjoy these woodland flowers. The Brownlows, the Talbots all used to collect. Inside it was all wood, built like a Norwegian house, with a long table in the middle, and rough Italian crockery on the shelves; we all sat round the big table and ate, the children with great eagerness.'

Conty Talbot wrote of one tea party in 1910:

'Geoffrey had been cooking all day at the Tea House in the beech woods'-for a picnic. 'There were little bunches of flowers, so typical of the Alfred Talbots'. Bridget Talbot turned to Conty and said 'You have always belonged to Geoffrey'. Conty did not agree. While she was moved by the efforts Geoffrey had made to impress her, 'in other ways he is so insensitive'. He was not to be put off. By 1911, Geoffrey had a motorcycle and was in even hotter pursuit. Conty went to a political meeting with Bridget *(Conty's father, Gustavus Adolphus Talbot, was Conservative MP for Hemel Hempstead)*. They had 'a long (and for Bridget) serious discussion about Geoffrey and his 'odd' devotion to me'. Things seemed to have come to a head at Ashridge at Christmas 1911. Conty describes Geoffrey having 'his eyes on me in a sort of anger: yes anger'. Geoffrey left for India at the beginning of January (1912) and we never really made friends again before he left'.
Conty also went to India in 1912 to see her brother, who was in the army, and perhaps to find a husband like others in the so called 'fishing fleet'. There she met a fifty one year old widower, Colonel William Sitwell. They were married later that year. She was half his age.
Four year later he was on the beaches at Gallipoli. His military reputation did not survive that disaster, and he was prematurely retired. The glamorous Colonel had become the out of work General, living with an increasingly bored wife in his crumbling castle at Barmoor, Northumberland, over three hundred miles away from Ashridge.

In those last years before the Great War there had been dramatic changes in Little Gaddesden as well. On the 26th January 1912, just after Geoffrey had left for India, his fifty nine year old mother, Emily Louisa Augusta, died without warning at Little Gaddesden

House of a cerebral haemorrhage. The coroner was informed by Humphrey. Then, less than 18 months later in June 1913, her husband, Alfred Talbot, died at the London and North Western Hotel in Holyhead returning from a visit to cousins in Ireland, where he had caught a cold. He had been laid up at Holyhead with pleurisy for some days and died of pneumonia compounded by heart problems. He was sixty five years old and was buried next to his wife in Little Gaddesden churchyard. *(His effects totalled £80,892.3.6d)*

The four Talbot children, Bridget, Humphrey, Geoffrey and Kathleen, were now orphans, and none of them had married. Indeed Bridget seemed to have no intention of doing so, but also seemed to have no idea of what else to do with her life. Career opportunities for women of her class were almost non-existant. They were expected to marry and deliver at least an heir and a spare. After that they should be gracious and witty hostesses at the Saturday to Monday weekends that filled up the country calendar. Whereas her brothers had been sent to Eton, and Humphrey had gone to Oxford, Bridget and Kathleen had been educated at home, partly in the schoolroom at the top of Little Gaddesden House. They were taught languages, music and art, and went on holidays to Italy and France, but neither there, nor in the great country houses they visited, had they found husbands. This was hardly yet a significant problem for the younger sister, but Bridget was now almost thirty and in most eyes firmly 'on the shelf'.

Just over a year after their father's death the wider world changed utterly as well. With the outbreak of the First World War the 'lights had gone out all over Europe'. Ashridge, like Belton, had become a military hospital and some of their friends were already in uniform in France. Indeed some would die before the year's end. Conty Talbot's brother, another Humphrey Talbot, was killed at Ypres in 1914, aged just twenty five. With a General and an Admiral for uncles, it was no surprise that all four Talbot children would feel they had to do their bit and join up. All would be scarred by the 'war to end all wars', and one of them would not survive it.

Chapter 2

Geoffrey's War

When war was declared Conty's frustrated suitor, Geoffrey Richard Henry Talbot, was twenty six and working for the East Indian Railway Company. He was born on the 29ᵗʰ March, 1888, and had been educated at boarding school at Westgate and then at Eton and, according to the Morning Post, had a 'great taste for mechanics'. He had been in British India since at least 1911 and, with his social contacts, must have had a very enjoyable, not to say privileged, time, with plenty of opportunity for riding horses and motorcycles as well as trains. Perhaps he was still in love with Conty because there is no record of another girl friend, let alone a fiancée. However, when the call to arms came he seems to have responded quickly and returned to England to enlist. Perhaps he was one of those scared that they would miss out on the glory, since many thought the war would be over by Christmas.

Of course he was a Talbot, whose ancestor, the 4th Earl of Shrewsbury, John Talbot, had been the most famous English commander in the latter stages of the Hundred Years War. John Talbot is a central character in Shakespeare's Henry V1th Part 1, where on his death Sir William Lucy says,

'Is Talbot slain, the Frenchman's only scourge,
Your Kingdom's terror and Black Nemesis'.

The French Bastard says of Talbot's son, a few lines earlier,
'How the young whelp of Talbot's, raging-wood,
Did flesh his puny sword in Frenchman's blood'.

Geoffrey did not have to look that far back for warlike inspiration of course, as he had an Admiral and a General for uncles. The latter, Uncle Reggie, who was also Geoffrey's godfather, ended his days as Major General the Honourable Sir Reginald Arthur James Talbot KCB CB, Commander of the Army of Occupation in Egypt and then Governor of Victoria, Australia. So the question was not would Geoffrey volunteer to fight, this was of course before conscription, but in what service? The cavalry would no doubt have been attractive but it had soon become clear that there was little role for mounted soldiers in the trenches of Flanders. However there was a new sort of cavalry — in the skies. Serious flying was hardly ten years old, indeed the first cross channel flight had only taken place in 1909. The aircraft's military role was uncertain. Initially planes were used for reconnaissance, aerial combat was unusual, and in any case it would be two years into the war before pilots were able to shoot through their propellers in line with their direction of flight. Until then they had to fire out of the side, or lean out and drop small bombs by hand. The pilots had no parachutes, and no protection from the elements. The higher they flew the colder it got. Many, including Geoffrey, wore large fur coats. Their great fear was of the plane catching fire and the pilot being burned to death, taking long agonizing minutes to spiral to earth. Some preferred to jump, others took along pistols to shorten their suffering

In fact in the early stages of the war the greatest danger to pilots came not from the enemy but from their own planes, whose engines would frequently malfunction. They had to be as brave, if not braver, than the Spitfire pilots a quarter of a century later, since the latter flew far more reliable aircraft. Geoffrey did not join the Royal Air Force, however, as it did not exist until near the end of the war.

In 1914 the choice for would be fliers was between the British Army's Royal Flying Corps, formed in 1912, and the Royal Naval Air Service, formed in late 1910. Geoffrey chose the latter and by 1915 he had his 'wings'. His Royal Aero Club Aviator's certificate examination was taken on a Maurice Farman BF plane at Chingford Essex on the 27th June 1915. Those early flying days, far from the front, seem to have been a lot of fun.

The first letter of Geoffrey's we have is from the central Flying School in Upavon, Wiltshire. (Telegrams 'Speedy,Upavon'.)
It is to a Miss Gough, and is dated the 2nd August 1915:-

Dear Miss Gough,
Many thanks for your letter. I am so glad that Bridget is coming down to stay with you but I am very doubtful about being able to come over to Amesbury *(also in Wiltshire)* as I am doing a workshop course next week and am also Emergency Pilot and am not supposed to leave the place at all.

Perhaps Miss Gough was a potential girl friend, because he went on:-

I might possibly be able to fly over though — but I don't know about landing near your house.
I will anyhow try to get them to let me fly in that direction some time after 5pm on Monday if the weather is suitable and will come down as low as possible,
Yours Sincerely,
Geoffrey R H Talbot.

Two weeks later he must have been assessed as ready for action because he had been moved from Upavon to Dover, where he was billeted at the Hotel Burlington.
From there he wrote to his sister Bridget, nicknamed Pussy, on the 3rd September 1915:-

Dearest Pussy,
Just a line to say that it is uncertain when we go to Dunkirk but probably in two or three weeks or less-I am at present in No 5 Squadron and found I knew practically everyone in it, as some are from Chingford, some from Upavon, and there is one man who was at Portsmouth.

Apparently we are not going out as a squadron but in two or three lots. The first lot is just going out and I believe I shall be in the third, but it is all very vague.

We live at the hotel and come up here to the station morning and afternoons and one of us stops here every night.

When we go to France, I believe it is for two months — one month bomb dropping and one month's reconnaissance and then one month in England out of which one gets 14 days leave-

If you would like to come down to the Burlington for 2 or 3 days let me know.

We get more time off here than at Upavon and you could live in the same place as I.

We go into khaki when we get over the other side so my old uniform will come in handy.

I hope to get 2 or 3 days leave before we go. Please send this on to K *(his other sister Kathleen)* — I got a letter from her yesterday and am writing to her about that day off.

Your Loving,

Geoffrey R H Talbot.

One day that summer Bridget, who was staying at Belton, received a telegram — reply paid.

Have got night off can you dine go theatre tonight. Wire Piccadilly Hotel quickly Geoffrey.

Bridget presumably had to drop everything and jump on a train to London. It's a measure of the closeness of brother and sister that Geoffrey thought she would. That early autumn Geoffrey seemed to be in high spirits. His godfather and uncle, General Sir Reggie, wrote to his niece K, on the Sept 25th 1915, from the Empire Hotel, Bath, where he was undertaking a cure.

I was able to run down to Dover to see Geoffrey fly. He does it beautifully and I felt very proud of him and I am sure he will distinguish himself if he gets the chance. He is as keen as mustard...

(Reggie seems to have become a surrogate father to the family of his deceased brother.)

Most of Geoffrey's surviving letters were written to his younger sister K. They were mainly addressed to her at the War Hospital, Clopton, Stratford Upon Avon where she was nursing. On October 4th he wrote to her from Dover:-

Dearest K,
Am just off to Dunkirk direct from here. <u>Very</u> many thanks for the gloves which will be very useful. I changed the pair you sent again as I found the gauntlets were not big enough to go over my leather coat etc. Hayford sent me another pair and said there was no difference in price.
Thank you v much for them.
Much love,
Your loving,
Geoffrey R H Talbot.

K was obviously deeply worried, as she should have been, given the appalling casualty rate among pilots.

Earl Brownlow, 'Uncle Addy', wrote to his niece on October 8th from Ashridge.

My darling Kathleen,
I have been a long time writing but my thoughts have so often been full of you darling. I know you will have felt deeply about dearest Geoffrey's going off, but it is so splendid of him to do so and he must have worked so hard to fit himself for this splendid work and so efficiently that one feels one <u>dares</u> not let oneself (?) with anxiety. But we can and ought to pray with bravery for our darling boy to be held up by the 'everlasting wings'.

Much of the rest of the letter is difficult to read but the Earl's love for Kathleen and Geoffrey shines through. Their uncle signed off, 'Your loving AB'.

After Geoffrey had flown over to France it was evidently K's job to keep her brother well supplied with treats. On the 19th October, 1915, he wrote from:-
British Expeditionary Force
No 1 Wing
Royal Naval Air Station, Dunkerque, France
do GPO London

Dear K,
Thank you very much for your various letters — the Bystander and an enormous parcel of food from Fortnum and Mason —
I am sorry not to have written to you sooner but it is somewhat difficult to get letters written here. It was wicked of you to send me all those things from Fortnum and M. but they will be very useful if we go out ahead or sleep in ditches-as I believe we sometimes do — otherwise the food is quite eatable here and we often go into Dunkerque and dine there — I blessed your gloves the other day when I was up on a patrol and thoroughly cold! They were capital. There is very little that I can tell you as of course we cannot say anything about what we do. I managed to smash a machine yesterday —my engine gave out and I came down plosh on Dunkerque beach and turned upside down! No damage to myself, but spoilt the look of machine absolutely. Now must stop as post is going.
Let me know if you get this —have ordered Bystander, Tatler, Punch and Daily Mail and Mirror regularly.
Much love,
Your Loving Geoffrey R.H.Talbot

PS You might send this to B — in case I can't write for a day or two.

(Throughout the war K seems to have copied the letters sent to her by her brothers and sister for distribution among family and friends).

K obviously took her shopping duties seriously because less than a week later Geoffrey was acknowledging receipt of more culinary delights:-

Dearest K,

Just a hurried line to thank you v — much for your letter of the 16th and for <u>excellent</u> cheese, sweets and marmalade — I haven't eaten the last yet but I know the make of old!

The weather to-day has been awful —wind and rain nearly the whole time and it is blowing like fury now — we were expecting our marquees, in which some of the machines are left, to blow over at any minute, but so far they have stood up — I am afraid I've no news that I can tell you as I have to be up at 4.45 and am sleeping in a hut on the aerodrome ready for the Boches. I will go and get some sleep.

Much love

Your Loving,

Geoffrey RH Talbot

K's shopping expeditions continued, indeed they appear to have become more ambitious and expensive. Britain might have been beginning to feel the effects of the German's U Boat campaign which severely reduced food imports and brought the country near to starvation, but in late 1915, if you could afford it, luxuries were still available.

6th November, 1915

Dearest K,

Thank you very much for your letter — And for marron glaces, truffles and foies gras — also a Strand magazine —You are wicked to keep on sending so many things - The socks will be most useful when they arrive as it is getting very cold in the air now.

We have had a good deal of excitement the last day or two — more than that I cannot say!

This morning 'somewhere in Europe', I chased an old Boche in the air but he was too quick for me and got away.

There has been a lot of rain lately, with a fine day or two in between-and the aerodrome has been more or less under water and it is messy work slopping about in it— There is usually a regular shower bath all around the machine when one takes off.

I hope your wrist is going on all right and not giving trouble, it was probably good for you having a rest.

Have you done anything more about coming out to France? If you are satisfied with Clopton (*the hospital near Stratford upon Avon where Kathleen was working*) I would think you would do much better to stop there-

Much love. Your Loving, Geoffrey RH Talbot

By 7th December, 1915, Geoffrey was back in England, and keen to see his sisters. He wrote to Bridget from the Burlington Hotel, Dover:-

Dearest Pussy,

According to present arrangements I get 10 days leave from the 16th and in the meantime we can do more or less as we like and needn't be up at the aerodrome most of the time, so would you and K like to come here for a few days — Possibly though K's arm won't be well enough but consult her and let me know.

Lambe is still here! Leslie has gone on leave.

We don't know if the Talbot children met up, but on New Year's Eve, 1915 Geoffrey was still staying in Dover at the Burlington Hotel and writing to his elder sister, Bridget, thanking her for Christmas presents:-

Dear Pussy,

<u>Very</u> many thanks for books and some excellent toffee which arrived the other day, also for many letters.

I'm afraid I haven't got you anything yet but will do so in London. All being well I hope to arrive at Belton (*the Brownlows' house in Lincolnshire*) tomorrow Saturday evening although it is not absolutely certain yet.

The war was not over by Christmas 1915 let alone 1914, as many had thought it would be, and now all the Talbot children were involved. Many of their friends, and some family, had already been killed. They must have doubted whether all four of them would survive, and the war was coming closer to home. The German bombers were starting to get through. Even central London was not safe.

Geoffrey had seen many of his pilot friends killed, sometimes in action, more often when their aircraft's engines failed. He can have had no doubt that the odds were against him surviving.

It must have been strange New Year at Belton. In 1915 Lord Brownlow had offered the Park for the war effort and it became the home depot and training ground of the Machine Corps, so the noise of rapid gun fire would have been as regular as the cock crows, and would have provided an uneasy background to the croquet. The Brownlows' other home at Ashridge was being used as a military hospital and its grounds for army training, overseen by Colonel Wheatley, the Agent, whose own son was in the front line.

The Talbots' parents were not at Belton of course. They had died just before the war, and now the children's aunt, Countess Adelaide Brownlow, was obviously ailing.

The lights had gone out over Europe and they were dimming at Belton and in Little Gaddesden. In twelve months time who would be left?

After the New Year break Geoffrey was soon back in harness. It should not be thought that Dover was a safe posting. More than half the pilots who died in WW1 died in training. If they ever got to the front they lasted on average a mere eleven days. In France or England it required great courage just to get into a plane and turn on the engine. In the evenings one might eat and drink well, and then sleep in clean sheets, but next morning your courage would be severely tested as you put yourself in harm's way simply by trying to take off. Nursing in Stratford Upon Avon Kathleen was in much less physical danger but the mental strain must have been considerable for such a young girl and a poisoned arm was giving her a lot of pain.

Burlington Hotel, Dover
20.1.16

Dearest K,

Many thanks for your letter. I will send B(*ridget*)'s.P(*ost*) Card on to Aunt Doobit *(Uncle Reggie's wife)*

Four of us have just been up to London to fly some machines back from Chingford but they weren't ready and the weather was so bad so we were sent back by train after waiting 4 days!

We hope to go back again!

I haven't heard anything of any Zepp raid on Canterbury, so I don't supposed it happened....

I hope the arms are all right.

Much love,

Your loving Geoffrey RH Talbot

The Zeppelin raids were beginning to cause great concern, if not panic, in London. Before 1914 the British believed that being an island gave them protection from invasion and war, the sea was their saviour, but suddenly bombs were dropping on central London. They were unprecedented, unexpected and lethal.

At the start of the war the German Army had seven military Zeppelins which had a maximum speed of 136 mph and could operate at a height of 4,250 metres. They were equipped with five machine guns and could carry 4,400 lbs of bombs.

The first Zeppelin raid on London took place on 31st May, 1915. It killed twenty eight people and injured sixty more. Later, Yarmouth, King's Lynn, Edinburgh, Gravesend, Sunderland, the Midlands and the Home Counties were all hit. By the end of May 1916 at least five hundred and fifty civilians had been killed by German Zeppelins. Pessimists now believed that 'The bomber will always get through'. Those tasked with stopping some of the bombers, like Geoffrey, were beginning to come in for criticism. Why couldn't they shoot down the Zeppelins and the Taubes, Germany's first bomber aircraft, before they reached their targets? Geoffrey had now to defend the skies over Kent, as well as training pilots, in between tours of duty in France.

Burlington Hotel, Dover
2 February 1916

Dearest K,

Sorry not to have written sooner. It was quite exciting the night the Taube came. I woke up to hear bombs going off all round (*one fell quite close to the Burlington*) and we tore up to the aerodrome but no one went up as the Taube had got away by then. The next day when they came again, 2 or 3 of our machines went up, and one man got within about 100 yards of a Taube just as he was going into a cloud and gave him 47 rounds in his tail, but not with much effect apparently — I didn't go up that day as my machine wasn't ready but the next day or thereabouts Germans were said to be coming over 'in increasing numbers' and I took an observer up with a repeating rifle and an automatic pistol but we couldn't find anything to kill-and again another day when two Taubes were said to be coming from Deal, also with no luck though.

Monday night we were all on the qui vive for the Zepps but they seem to have confined themselves to the Midlands —

Sunday I went for a flit in one of our airships for the first time — It felt very slow after an aeroplane.

Verner — the man Pussy was asking about, took me up and we went over Folkestone. I am still instructing here and we don't know yet when we go back but I expect not for a week or two as the sheds etc for the new aerodrome have only just gone over — Leslie and I are trying to get to the new aerodrome near Belton (*the Brownlow's Lincolnshire home*) for a bit in the meantime, but I don't suppose it will come off.

George still remains with me after all. His main grievance was, apparently, that I cursed him outside the Piccadilly Hotel one day and thus offended his dignity! So he told me he purposely didn't get up in the mornings for the next few days by way of reprisal! He is working much better now and the row has woken him up. Longmore has gone back to sea owing to some trouble at Dunkerque — apparently not his fault. He has given me a good character while I was under him — probably to my knowing Majorie!

I am getting to know some people round here, through Aunt Margaret, but nowadays it is very difficult to get away at all.

I enclose various letters from B. Please circulate them and return mine in due course — I'm afraid I didn't send yours on to H, (*his elder brother Humphrey*) but enclose it now.

Please send my letter (this) on to him.

I have just got a brand new machine for night flying in case of attack by Zepps etc.

Much love, Your Loving, Geoffrey RH Talbot

Burlington Hotel, Dover
11th February 1916
Dearest K

Thank you for two letters which I got yesterday on my return from Chingford where I had flown, with another man as passenger, via Redhill and Hendon the day before.

I brought another machine back via Tilbury and Sheerness. We started back the same evening but it was so thick when we got near the Thames that we went back to Chingford and started again the next day.

Do you remember Viney? He started off in another machine a day or two before, smashed up at Brooklands and then, just as he was starting from Chingford in the other machine he was to bring back, smashed that and turned upside down!

Very bad luck — however he wasn't hurt.

I enclose another letter from B which please return.

I don't suppose I shall be able to get away again till just before we go out, when we may get 2 or 3 days. It is a pity you can't come down here for a few days —

In haste. Your Loving,
Geoffrey RH Talbot

Burlington Hotel, Dover

2 March 1916 (*written in pencil, not ink as is usual*)
Dearest K,
Thanks very much for your letter and for B's to Aunt Addy
(*Countess Brownlow*) which I will send on to her. I have been in
bed since Monday with a go of flue or something very like it, but
I hope to get up to-morrow or the next day all being well. I have
got a funny old Fleet Surgeon looking after me —He's lost his
stethoscope, or never had one, so he sticks his hairy old face all
over my chest and back to listen to my inner workings with the
result that I am always on the point of having a giggling fit!
Yes, it was very sad about poor Rosher. It happened about half
a mile from the aerodrome and I am inclined to think something
went wrong with him and not the machine, although it is very
difficult to tell. They buried him here today. I am glad I didn't
actually see it happen, although I was there immediately afterwards.
He must have been killed instantaneously.
I flew over Mrs Montague's house at Sandwich on Monday
morning but don't know whether they spotted me — I had told
them that I would come and drop oranges on them!
When do you go back to Clopton?
I hope you may have a good bit longer — Give Aunt Doobit
my love.

Burlington Hotel, Dover
15th march 1916

Dearest K,

No news yet as to when we go out and as there only 5 of us
(*war pilots*) here now, it may be some days yet. I have just
discovered that you paid for the sitting-room when you were
down here and am livid with rage in consequence as I told them
to charge it to me — I enclose cheque for this and for what you
paid into Coutts for the time before and I think the amount is
about right, but I haven't got my pass book here. Let me know if
it's not right.

It's filthy weather here. Thick mist on the aerodrome nearly all the time.
Much love

Burlington Hotel, Dover
21st March 1916
Dearest K,
Thanks for letter.
We had an exciting time here on Sunday.
Leslie and I were just going down to lunch when we saw a strange looking machine overhead which someone who had looked through a telescope said was a Hun.
So we leaped into two machines and began to give chase — he got off in about 4 minutes and I in about 6. I started straight for the sea but just when I got over the valley my infernal engine began to fail and I very nearly had to land on the top of the town, however I managed to get it to pick up again for two or three minutes and got above the cliff between Dover and Folkestone and was just beginning to turn out to sea again when it failed again and I had to come down. I tried to get onto the only level strip of ground up there, but it was too small so I jumped a railing and crashed into a barbed wire entanglement outside the fort!
I very nearly landed on one of their guns — I damaged the machine rather badly but got off all right except for a small cut on my forehead.
It <u>was</u> annoying as I think I should have had a very good chance of catching him if my engine hadn't failed — I went up to the place yesterday to have a look at it and was surrounded by tommies with bits of the propeller which I had to autograph!
It was splendid Bone (from Westgate) getting one of them as he has done a lot of good work in France. It was quite by chance that he was there. I don't think I told you when I last wrote that Lambe put me forward for my second stripe about ten days ago, so I hope it will come off.
I wish they would give us good machines to fly as then we might have a chance to get a Hun

—The one I was on had failed 4 times in 3 days just before it failed with me. The result is we can't catch them and people say we are no use.

Leslie followed one of them right over to Belgium but couldn't get up to his height — He had tea at Dunkerque and came back. Much love.

Geoffrey was getting increasingly irritated by suggestions that pilots like him were not up to the job of defending the country. Five days later he wrote to his uncle and godfather Reggie, the Victorian war hero, who had many friends in high places and around his dinner table.

Burlington Hotel, Dover, 26th March, 1916

Dear Uncle Reggie,
Thank you for your letter.
We had quite an exciting time last Sunday and the allegations against us in the papers are mainly lies — As it happened, every available pilot was at the aerodrome when the Germans came and no one was then at lunch .... It was maddening to see the Germans disappearing and being unable to do anything. I think if my engine had been all right I should have had a fair chance of getting up to them —
That d-d machine had failed 4 times in the previous 3 days with other pilots and I wasn't the least surprised when it did so again.
You ask if I have any suggestions to make about the air service. I have many and could start with several for Dover as a beginning, but as letters are sometimes censored here I cannot put them in writing.
I heard from Bridget again the other day — she seems to contemplate stopping in Italy for some time. I was told unofficially that Lambe sent in my name for a second stripe about 3 weeks ago, so I hope I may get it soon.
I believe they are still not quite ready for us in France so we may be here for some time yet — perhaps a week or two....

Please give Aunt Margaret my love,
Your Affectionate,
Geoffrey RH Talbot.

On the 2nd April 1916, he again wrote to his godfather describing how difficult it was to navigate without a clear view of the ground below and of course, with no modern navigational aids.

Burlington Hotel
Dear Uncle Reggie,
Thank you for sending me on Bridget's letter which I now return. I eventually got off on Friday. I started from Chingford before lunch but when I got somewhere near the Thames it was so foggy that I could hardly see anything so went back and landed. I had another attempt after lunch and found it just as bad but thought I might as well go on so I did and got properly lost somewhere near the Medway. Eventually I saw a strange aerodrome below me and came down to where I was. It turned out to be Detling near Maidstone so I wasn't so very far off my course. I then went on and landed all right at Westgate and flew another machine back to Dover via Folkestone.
You will be glad to know I am now a Flight Lieut. It was in the paper this morning. I am v glad Leslie has got his also.
I had another smash yesterday and turned upside down so am feeling rather as if I had been rolled down a hill in a barrel today! It was my fault and not the machine's on this occasion as I bounced when landing and she turned right over.

Geoffrey must have realised that his luck was bound to run out soon, but there is no sign of undue strain in his letters, nor a misplaced sense of immortality. Uncle Reggie could only hope and pray for his survival. With no child of his own, the old General seems to have been particularly close to his younger nephew, particular since his brother, Geoffrey's father Alfred, had died.
Geoffrey wrote and told both his sisters about his promotion, with obvious pride, and also about the crashes, but without much detail. This was his letter to Bridget, of the 4th April

Burlington Hotel, Dover
Dear Pussy,
Thank you very much for your birthday letters and others, also for some <u>excellent</u> sweets from Fuller's and a seductive cake.
You will be glad to hear that I have got my promotion and am now a Flight-Lieut. Leslie and two other men here have also got it. I very nearly beat them as old Lambe sent in my name for special promotion as well as on the quarterly promotion list, so if the special list had come out before the other one I should have become senior to several people. We are still expecting to go to France at anytime but they are not quite ready for us otherwise we should have gone long before this. Zepps have been over England at least three nights running now. It was splendid one being brought down at the mouth of the Thames, but a great pity they could not tow her in intact....
I had another smash a few days ago, owing to making a bouncy landing, and the machine turned upside down.
I didn't damage myself however, except for one or two cuts and bruises.
Let me know if you want anything sent out to you (in Italy).
Much love,
Your Loving Geoffrey R H Talbot

We have only one more letter from Geoffrey. It was written two months later and sent to his younger sister.

Please address all correspondence as follows
No 1 Wing, Royal Naval Air Service,
do G PO London
6th June, 1916

Dearest K,
Many Thanks for your letter
I had a very pleasant fly over that Sunday. It only took about 23 minutes from shore to shore.
I found, as usual, when I got here that they didn't really want me! They had asked for me to replace another man who was going

home temporarily but in the meantime they decided to keep him here as well, so sent another man home instead.

There hasn't been much doing since I arrived but I think there will be plenty going on soon.

I enclose a letter from B which arrived yesterday. Please send it on to H when done with.

G. Bunn *(the manager of their Little Gaddesden estate)* came up to the aerodrome at Dover and saw me start the other day. I asked him what he thought of the various machines but he wouldn't commit himself!

I am glad to see the naval battle was not so bad for us as appeared at first and I hope we may get even better news in today's papers.

(Geoffrey is here referring to the Battle of Jutland, the only major surface naval battle of the war. In it the British lost more shipping and twice as many sailors as the German fleet. A disconcerted Admiral Beatty famously said "Something wrong with our bloody ships today".

The 'invincible' British navy appeared to have been defeated, but the German fleet returned to port and never came out again. The Royal Navy could be said to have lost the battle but won the sea war.)

Please don't bother about sending Sketch and Strand as we are now getting a fairly good supply on the mess.

From what I can see of things this (the old place) is a much better station than the new place I was originally going to.

You will be glad to hear that I got a glowing report from Dover.

Much love,

Your Loving,

Geoffrey RH Talbot

There was indeed no point in sending the Sketch or the Strand.

Twenty eight year old Geoffrey Talbot died a couple of weeks later when his plane crashed in Dover. It was said at the inquest that he had only arrived at the Dover station on the Thursday and was killed at 4pm that afternoon, having taken off in a Nieuport biplane with Air Mechanic Hampson, aged twenty three, who was also killed.

Both men were unconscious when help reached them and Geoffrey died, from multiple injuries, when he was being lifted into an ambulance. He had been flying for one year and two days.

After Geoffrey's death K must have received a number of letters of sympathy. A handful survive.

On July 3rd Evelyn H Barclay wrote from Runton Old Hall, Nr Cromer

My dear K,

Geoffrey was such a dear good friend of mine, his death has come quite a shock to me. Will you please accept my sincerest sympathy. What more can I say I don't know, but you will understand Kathleen, won't you that I feel for you more than I can ever write or tell you.

In deepest sympathy and I will mourn for a really good friend who will not be easily replaced.

Your very affectionate
Evelyn H Barclay

He wrote again three days later on July 6th having heard the funeral had already taken place.

My dear K,

I am very grateful for your letter which I received this morning but I feel it that I was not able to pay my last tribute possible to dear old Geoffrey, which I would have liked to. But I never knew, you see, that anything had happened except by the newspapers and I could not possibly get up in time. I owe this explanation to you, because he was such an old friend of mine and hence this is the last thing I could have done, if only I had known to show how much I appreciated his friendship.

Yours,
Evelyn

Another letter came on the 9th July, 1916 from Halls Croft, Stratford-On-Avon. A signature is missing, but it was possibly from K's aunt, Odeyne Hodgson, who ran Clopton Hospital where K had been working as a nurse.

Dearest K,

Thank you so much for your letter this morning. It was good of you to write and I was very glad to hear from you just how it happened. You must be very, very proud of him — it gives one joy to hear of such unflinching courage — and I know it must comfort your brave heart.

Dearest K, it is splendid of you to come back to Clopton — I expect you will find life easier while you are working, but the effort to begin anything again must be dreadful. Don't come till you know the convoy is here. Everyday that passes I know is a blessing to you now. I do hold your hand in spirit K darling — I think I know a little what you are going through, because I have had to face the possibility of the same grief for so long myself.

But you have the reality now and I do send you all my love and deepest sympathy each moment.

On July 11th 1916 Phyllis Leslie wrote from 11 Portland Place, London. She had just become the wife of the Leslie who served with Geoffrey.

Dear Miss Talbot,

It was very kind of you to bother to answer my letter, but I really didn't expect you to in all your deep sorrow. I hope when you and your sister are in London you will let me see you both. The above address will always find me. I wonder if you would let me know where I can get a photograph of the dear old man, as we so want to have one — anytime will do, when you feel more like writing.

Hoping you are all fairly well.

Yours very sincerely

Phyllis Leslie

Flight-Lieutenant G. R. H. Talbot was buried at Little Gaddesden. The funeral was conducted by his uncle, the Rev. F. H. Hodgson, and the Rev. E. Clark.

Humphrey, Bridget and Kathleen were all there, as was Uncle Reggie and Earl Brownlow, and many other relatives, including Cooie Lane.

Also present was Flt. Lt. and Mrs. Leslie and Flt. Lt Joyce.

So how exactly did Geoffrey die?

The report in the Morning Post of the 3rd of July 1916 said this:-

Flight-Lieutenant G. R. H. Talbot, Royal Naval Air Service, was killed instantaneously at Dover on June 29 in commencing a flight to France. The aeroplane was caught by a gust of wind, side-slipped, and was wrecked. The mechanic was also killed.

It went on to say that after joining the Service Geoffrey had rapidly become:-

....an expert and exceptionally enterprising and steady pilot. He had made many flights to and from France, whence he had returned only the previous day to that on which the accident occurred. He was a man of generous and affectionate disposition, very popular with his comrades, and the men under him, both in India and in the Air Service. He is mourned by a large circle of relations and friends.

Later that week the Coroner's Inquest was held. It was told that nothing was wrong with the aircraft and, while it was also said that the accident was no one's fault, the verdict could be read as suggesting that pilot error, in difficult circumstances, contributed to the crash. There was no suggestion that Geoffrey was taking evasive action to avoid hitting something on the ground.

There is a later, more heroic account, dated the 4th February 1921.

It was written by A.R.George who lived at St Aubins, Burgh Road, Aylsham:-

Dear (*There is no addressee*)

I consider it a privilege to be able to give you particulars of the aeroplane accident I witnessed at Dover in June 1916, which I afterwards learnt resulted in the death of Mr. Geoffrey Talbot.

Between five and six thousand of us (R.G.A.Recruits) were drilling on the Parade Ground at Fort Burgoyne, and you can imagine we were closely packed, when an aeroplane rose from behind the Fort and suddenly swooped down directly over the heads of the men drilling, so closely in fact that many fell on their faces to avoid being hit by the propellers, but the pilot in order to avoid what would have been a terrible catastrophe swerved sharply to the left, and the machine fell into a sunken road near the Fort.

There is no doubt that the machine would have landed in the thick of the men with terrible results but with safety to the two men in it, and it was freely admitted by all who witnessed it that the pilot lost his life in a most gallant attempt to avoid crashing amongst a dense mass of men.

I heard it said by the airman there, that air currents around Fort Burgoyne were very bad and this was probably the cause of the accident. From what I can remember, the two men were pinned under the machine and were picked up quite dead.

It may be some consolation to his relatives to know that Mr.Geoffrey Talbot gave his life in this heroic manner and I consider it an honour to give this testimony as an eye-witness of the sad affair.

I remain, Sincerely yours,

A.R.George

One wonders why this letter was written five years after the event. Was it for general circulation? If so why? Had someone suggested Geoffrey's poor flying had caused the accident? Or did some sympathetic friend, seeing how much Geoffrey's family and friends were still grieving, want to reassure them that he had died a hero?

Of course many such letters were written during and after the war. They usually assured relatives that their loved ones had died instantly and heroically, whether they had or not.

In this case it hardly seems to matter. With so many being killed by their flying machines, and after so many near misses of his own, Geoffrey Talbot was a hero simply to climb into his plane and turn on the engine, as he did time after time after time.

And he does seem to have been genuinely loved by his colleagues. Geoffrey Bromet wrote from No S Wing, R N AS, presumably to K:-

...my excuse for writing to you is, not so much to describe how your brother met with his death but to ask you to allow me to express my deepest sympathy with you in the irretrievable loss which you have sustained. It may be of some comfort to you to know how every officer and man, with whom he came into contact, looked up to him as a model of what an officer and an English gentleman should be.

For my part I can only say that I have never felt anybody's loss so much. As an officer he was invaluable to me, both by reason of his cheerfulness and energy; as a pilot his courage and willingness to undertake anything at anytime, set an example to younger pilots which, in itself, was sufficient to make him indispensable to me. As a pal I do not think I can better express my feelings than to say that he was a 'white man'. I valued his friendship more than most things in this world, although we had only known each other for three months, and we planned splendid times in the future.

To think that he, of all men, should be lost to this world when his prospects were so rosy and his assistance so valuable seems so cruel, and absolutely unnecessary.

Believe me,

Yours very sincerely, Geoffrey Bromet

Geoffey Talbot was buried on the 4th July, 1916, in Little Gaddesden churchyard alongside the grave of his parents, after the funeral service in the church of St Peter and St Paul where he had been baptised twenty eight years before. His log book is now at Kiplin Hall along with a certificate from King George V which was sent to his family. It read:-

He whom this scroll commemorates was numbered among those who, at the call of King and Country, left all that was dear to them, endured hardness, faced danger, and finally passed out of the sight of men by the path of duty and self-sacrifice, giving up their own lives that others might live in freedom.

Let those who come after see to it that his name be not forgotten.

Flight Lt. Geoffrey Richard Henry Talbot RN

(His friend Leslie survived the first war, and stayed in the air force until he retired in the 1930's. When World War 2 began Wing Commander Reginald.F.Leslie DSC DFC AFC Italian Bronze medal for Valour, rejoined his service and was killed in action over Tunisia on the 11th July, 1943, aged fifty two. Shortly before he died he gave a speech to help raise money for building more aircraft. Speaking of the Germans he said "They are an obscene people – they need killing". Perhaps he had seen too many of his friends die.)

In just over four years the family of the Alfred Talbots of Little Gaddesden had halved in size. Once there were six, now there were three, and there was no sign of an end to this 'war to end all wars', in which all three surviving children were now caught up, and still at risk.

Chapter 3

Bridget's Early War

When her younger brother Geoffrey was killed at Dover in the summer of 1916, Bridget Elizabeth Talbot was returning from Italy where she was serving with the 'Pro Italia' group on the Austria-Italian front, receiving and tending to soldiers wounded in the trenches before sending them back to base hospitals. She was thirty one years of age, born in Little Gaddesden on the 15th January, 1885.

In some ways Bridget must have welcomed the war, or at least the opportunities for action it gave her. When it started she was twenty nine, unmarried, and without a career.

A local historian who knew her, the vicar of Little Gaddesden, Howard Senar, wrote that she had attended a school for young gentlemen at Robin Hood House in the village with her brother, but there is no record of any higher education, unlike that enjoyed by her brothers.

No doubt there were governesses and trips abroad, but when she was eighteen she was travelling around Britain, spending almost every other weekend at one country house after another in the Edwardian heyday of Empire, surrounded, one assumes, by 'suitable' young men. None of them seemed to suit Bridget, or perhaps she found the idea of surrendering her freedom and promising to obey a husband extremely unattractive.

From birth she seems to have been stubbornly independent, a natural rebel, with a real social conscience. She rarely seemed to arrive anywhere on time and could be somewhat vague. Early photographs of her as a baby show a very determined face and she remained determined, and sometimes intimidating, all her life, albeit with a great sense of humour.

Conty (Talbot) Sitwell gives a glimpse of B's independent nature when she wrote in her diary in 1905 about going to Ashridge. 'Bridget was to have been there but (naturally) had gone away somewhere'. A cousin, Barbara Cassell, formerly Lane, said that 'relations of her generation found her fun but not to be relied upon-one cousin said she wouldn't even buy a bale of hay from her! However, she was pretty when young and she was always popular with children — who perhaps were encouraged to be slightly naughty'...

Until the war Bridget's organisational abilities were confined to her village. In 1910 she founded the Little Gaddesden Scout Group, becoming its President. She soon installed her brother Humphrey as Treasurer and persuaded Uncle Addie (*Lord Brownlow*) to hand over the village armory at no 27 LG for their use.

She organised concerts to raise money for equipment for the scouts and later wrote a history of her Group. Twenty eight boys joined and camps, parades and rallies were held. Eminent visitors to the armory left their signatures in a book. On the 8th December, 1912, the Chief Scout, Robert Baden-Powell came, together with the Duke of Norfolk, a member of the Scout Council.

In 1913 they held a Field day with scout troops from surrounding areas, in which they tried to get a 'convoy' through Ashridge Park to Thunderdell Lodge, which represented a fort under siege. Bridget was in the thick of it, directing affairs sitting on a donkey. Soon the real thing would be upon them and they would no longer be playing at war. Some of those young boy scouts would never return home. Perhaps anticipating the conflict, in July 1914 Bridget had taken a Red Cross examination in 'proficiency in home nursing'.

On August 3rd 1914, Lord Kitchener was having tea in the loggia at Ashridge House with Lady Brownlow when he received a telegram from the War Office summoning him back to London Bridget wrote in the scout book:-

War between England and Germany was declared on August 4th. The LG Troop are proud to record that their former Assistant

Scoutmaster, Bernard Phillips is now serving his country on board HMS Implacable. George Pinnock is on HMS Powerful (*he was killed in action aged sixteen*) and A.Whitman (*killed in action aged twenty two*) is with the Territorial. The Chief Scout has called on all scouts to be ready to help. Fourteen boys offered their help.

Bridget was determined to help as well, but of course could not serve in the men only front line. What else could she do?

The immediate cause of Britain's entry in the war was Germany's invasion of 'plucky little Belgium'. The Kaiser was attempting to win the war in the west against France as quickly as possible to avoid a prolonged war on two fronts, and wanted to take a short cut through Belgium. His plan of campaign assumed knocking out France within a few weeks and then turning German might East, on Russia.

Belgium had the misfortune to be in the way, refused to let the German armies through, and was promptly invaded. Its armies were quickly pushed back. The British Expeditionary Force, the BEF, cavalry to the fore, advanced to defend its ally but was quickly driven back as well, and then what were thought to be temporary trenches were dug all through Flanders to the sea.

Tens of thousands of Belgian refugees, along with the country's royal family, fled to Britain. They were mainly women and children, and appeals went out for accommodation. They brought with them tales of atrocities, of rape and the murder of women and children. Many of these stories were undoubtedly true.

In trying to keep to their very ambitious timetable, the Germans adopted a policy of Schreklichkeit (frightfulness), intended to cow the population by the destruction of property and the execution of civilians. Louvain, with its famous library of priceless medieval manuscripts, was burned in reprisal for alleged civilian resistance.

A Belgian Refugee Committee was set up in Britain and Bridget became a member in October, 1914. Depots were opened at Alexandra Palace and Earl's Court in London to house the refugees. Perhaps some were taken in at Little Gaddesden house.

There was certainly room as many of the male servants there, and at the Talbots' London home in Cadogan Gardens, had quickly enlisted in the armed services.

It was soon clear that German U Boats would be a major threat to British shipping and that the country, highly dependent on imports, needed to become more self sufficient. So Bridget organised the Little Gaddesden Cooperative Allotment Scheme. Her 'Who's Who' entry said:-

In 1914 started the cultivation of co-operative gardens on wasteland. Ministry of Agriculture later adopted the scheme all over the country.

At Kiplin Hall is a certificate presented to Bridget, signed by Lord Selborne, the Minister for Agriculture and by Walter Runciman, which says: 'Every woman who helps in agriculture during the war is as truly serving her country as the man who is fighting in the trenches or on the sea'.

What more could she do? By 1915 she undertook further training as a nurse and a year later she set out to join the 'Pro Italia' group on the Austria-Italian front, receiving, tending and feeding wounded soldiers before sending them on to base hospitals. She and her sister K had holidayed in northern Italy in 1912, and she had loved the people, the countryside, the Venetian coastline and the culture. Bridget could also speak the language a little, so when Mrs. Henry Watkins asked for young ladies to help with the mobile canteens she was taking to the Italian Front Bridget volunteered. When exactly did she go out? Bridget's handwriting was dreadful, and someone, probably her sister Kathleen, typed up some of her letters for circulation to family and friends. In the first of these transcribed letters in our possession, Bridget writes from Paris on the way to the Italian front. It is dated January, 1915, but as Italy did not come into the war until May 23rd of that year the date must be a mistake. We believe it was 1916. This would seem to be confirmed by her entry in 'Who's Who' which gives 1916-1919 as the dates for her involvement with the Anglo Italian Red Cross.

There is also that letter from Geoffrey Talbot to Ms.Gough, dated the 21st August, 1915, and sent from the Central Flying School, Upavon, Wilts. which says 'I am so glad that Bridget is coming down to stay with you'.... and later that he is 'very doubtful about coming over to Amesbury' (*to see them*). So Bridget was definitely in England in the summer of 1915.

In April, 1918, while in Rome, Mrs. Watkins wrote an account of her organisation's work for the War Office. It is now in the Imperial War Museum.

Here is an extract:-

When Italy came into the war, I sent a message to General Cadorna asking if a group of English ladies could be of help in feeding the wounded on the Italian front. General Cadorna's answer was immediate and most cordial and fixed upon Cervignano and Cormons as suitable places.

The necessary funds were subscribed by my friends and others who were lovers of Italy and the subscription list was headed by the 'Pro Italia' society in London whose name we adopted, and whose secretary, Count De La Feld, undertook to be my treasurer, while the Italian Ambassador kindly agreed to be our patron. All of the funds went to the work as we paid our own expenses.

At Cervignano we were allotted billets and at the station a charming chalet was built for our work consisting of a kitchen, a big receiving room, just opposite the platform where the wounded were entrained, Cervignano being the railhead. Here we stayed from September 1915 until October 1917 with the exception of three weeks in May 1917 when after the heavy and repeated bombardment of the town we received an order from Headquarters of the 3rd Artillery to move into other quarters in an outlying village. From there we were able to continue our canteen work at a temporary entraining.

When the Austrians retook the town in October 1917 our chalet was burnt to the ground just before their entry.

Our principal work was feeding and tending the wounded in the trains, administering first aid in our chalet, and assisting the Italian Red Cross in the station.

We also undertook a second 'Posto di Restoro' at San G. di Manzano close to Cormons, another railhead'.

At the beginning of 1916, probably for the first time, Bridget set out for the Italian Front and Mrs. Watkins' headquarters.

PARIS
Tuesday
Jan.11-1915 (*we think 1916*)
We got here about midnight after a fearful journey of waiting about. There was a great delay at Folkestone, as quantities of troops were going off. We saw them all marching past and embark.

Before setting out Bridget had made sure she would have a privileged passage, if not a comfortable one:-

The letter Kitchener gave me was most effective at Folkestone and we were treated like royalty, going on board after everyone else and having our passports looked at in the military place instead of in the crowd, where we should have had to wait hours; and being seen off by officials! It was a filthy little boat — a dirty cabin very crowded and not a sheltered corner anywhere on deck and waves coming over everywhere, bitterly cold and a tremendous roll. I stayed up on deck and got thoroughly wet.... I heard a gun or bomb here at 1.30, but we have not found out yet what it was. I was too exhausted to get up and see, but I heard other people opening windows and calling out. We go on tonight to Milan, getting there late tomorrow, and then on at 7.30am.

In 1914 it had been far from clear on whose side Italy would fight. She had been a member of the Triple Alliance with Austria-Hungary and Germany, but had not declared war in August 1914 as they had done. So Allied diplomats had begun courting Italy, attempting to bring her in on their side. They succeeded. In the Treaty of London of the 26th April 1915 Italy renounced her obligations to the Triple Alliance and on May 23rd declared war on Austria-Hungary. However, Italian public opinion was heavily divided, so why did Italy change sides?

With the Allies help, Italy hoped to gain Cisalpine Tyrol, the Austrian Littoral and South Tyrol. She launched a surprise offensive intending to move quickly and capture several Austrian cities, but the war soon became bogged down into trench warfare similar to the Western front in France, but often high in the Italian Alps.

Bridget Talbot also kept a diary from January to June 1916 whilst serving as a volunteer during the Allied battle for Trieste. She was behind the lines waiting for trains to bring back the wounded but it was hardly a safe posting.

Diary - Wed Jan 19th 11 o'c :-
Hut cleaned and polished when bomb crash as aeroplane drops a bomb less than 15 yards off in the hospital grounds...

Diary Jan 20 Thurs
Mrs.Watkins and I went to lunch at Villa Trenta and saw the English Field Hosp. We went into one of the wards to see one of the ambulance drivers Ld. Ossulston who had appendicitis. He was in a most ghastly ward-one man opposite raving mad and others groaning and screaming when their wounds were dressed. He said it was awful at night as directly he tried to go to sleep the man next door with both legs off began screaming and woke him up.

Letter - Jan. 22nd 1915 *(Should be 1916)* :-
We are in a very dangerous position here, as we have no dug-out and they always try and bomb the station. I suppose when some of us are killed they will begin making one. Being British, it is beneath our dignity to ask for one! We have 'wounded' trains loaded up here with 200 to 300 men straight out of the trenches

most days. They very often haven't had food for two or three days, and come down in the most awful state. We also make things for the Field Hospitals which are very poorly equipped. We have so far done our own cooking, but now the General has sent us his Mess waiter to help, and he does a good deal.

But alongside the danger and hard work there were also snatched moments of pleasure:-

We had a delightful evening yesterday: we three and four of the English ambulance drivers — Alford, the poet, Seabrooke, the artist, Dr Ashley, the Roman archaeologist — went to an Italian house and a Pernaza sergeant, the Roman opera singer, sang — a magnificent voice. He was accompanied by Count Gvaoina, a great-grandson of Wagner, although an Italian.
The accompaniment was not what it might have been as Gvaoina was very exhausted, having been under heavy fire a few hours before.
It felt very strange: the opera singing going on and the guns booming away outside and the audience consisting of us and lots of Italian officers.
Do write and tell me the English news. We hear practically none hear and letters and papers take anything from 12 days to 6 weeks to arrive, and then very often get lost.

Bridget was not impressed by the Italian upper classes:-

They are mostly neutral and some even quite openly pro-German as they say the war would have been over by now if they had gone over to Germany and they think they would have got greater advantages for Italy by joining the other side. They - the Upper Classes-are <u>not</u> putting their back into it yet though I think the <u>people</u> are. One realises what a near shave it was that Italy came in with us at all, simply because the people liked us.

Bridget here is being a little naïve. The Italian Government joined the Allies because of the Austria-Hungarian territories it was promised in a post war settlement. In effect the Allies bribed the Italians with the promise of land. However Bridget had no doubts about the justice of the cause or the value of her war effort:-

It is undoubtedly of great use our being here, from the English point of view, as 300 to 400 starving wounded men every day get their first food from an English Posto, and are not likely to forget it in a hurry...

She had no illusions about the horrors of war in the mountains, they were all too evident:-

.....It is a fearful job getting the wounded down from the trenches — they have to be dragged part of the way or brought on mules — and then ambulances-and many die on the way.

At this early stage she was optimistic about an early Italian victory:

.....I hear there may be fighting again in a few days, but the big advance will only be in a month's time I expect. It is all arranged that we are to have horses to ride, and make a triumphal entry into Goritzia!

She never made that triumphal entry. The Italian offensives were easily repulsed, but B's career was prospering. Within a month of arriving in northern Italy, on Sunday Feb 6th,1916, Bridget wrote home that she had been promoted:-

....I have now been appointed field telephonist and railway officer to the English Hospital and have to find out and arrange every day how many wounded are to go down by the trains, which saves their having to send a man and a motor down every evening. Also, I have taken on the receiving and distribution of bales of much needed goods for the various hospitals from the Committees at Venice, Milan and Florence ...
I had my first early train yesterday, which I had to do alone with only Speranza to help. The alarm didn't go off, but by great good

luck I woke up at five and went down in the pitch dark to the canteen to get things ready, and the train went at six. It felt very weird and warlike feeding the wounded soldiers by the light of a lantern with the sunrise beginning over the mountains.

The Austrian bombing continued and on Feb 14th, 1916 she wrote in her diary that she had taken refuge in the officers' mess:-

For half an hour we waited in the dark and cold wondering when the next bomb wd fall on the ammunition sheds at the back of the house and blow us to the other side of nowhere. One did fall on them but did not explode. We certainly do live on the edge of a volcano here......

I remember being terrified that the Italian officers should see that my teeth were chattering hard and think I was afraid! However they seem to have been enormously impressed because I suggested going out to see if there were any wounded! It is an awful responsibility that everything one does is put down to England. It certainly adds zest to life to think one is really a cog in the giant machinery of the Gt war for liberty, justice and a representative of England.

The next day she wrote in a letter that:-

....a kind old Major said he hoped we were not afraid and it was quite all right. Still very sleepy, I felt furious that they should think that we English could be afraid, and I turned to him fiercely and said, in bad Italian, 'Signor Mazzoire, the English do not know what fear is'. They laughed a great deal over this the next morning.

Bridget was the recipient of inside information on the conduct of the war. Her aunt Lady Margaret, wife of Uncle Reggie the military hero, wrote that she had had Kitchener, Lord Chelmsford and Lord Montague to dine, and that troops were being hurriedly brought back from Egypt to France.

Meanwhile her cousin Conty (*Talbot*) Sitwell, wife of one of the Generals fired over the disaster of Gallipoli, wrote to say that leading parliamentarians like Sir Edward Carson were working for an enquiry into that ill-fated expedition. Conty obviously hoped it would exonerate her husband.

By late February the weather had changed for the worse:-

Letter - Feb 23rd 1916:-

.....simply deluges of rain and snow today, and the roads knee deep in mud. It somehow feels more in keeping with the War than the hot Italian sun and blue skies we have had lately — but the poor wretches must be having a ghastly time, especially on the mountains, where they can't dig themselves in properly.

We had some wretched men in this morning, their boots coming to bits and soaked through, and filthy after two months in the trenches, and the last bit in the front line, where most of their regiment have been cut to bits this week. There is one place where the English ambulances go where the trenches are on the edge of a precipice at the top of a snow mountain, and everything and everybody, including the wounded, have to be run up and down several thousand feet with a rope and a basket. The big guns have begun again ...

We have had our third invitation today for the night of the 25th, when the Austrians have dropped papers to say they are going to shell this place.

(*The invitations were to share shelters.*)

No 1 was at the Stationmaster's cellar which is full of rats.

No 2 to the officers' mess on the lowest floor of our farm, and

No 3 to the English hospital.

However, if this weather continues, we shan't have to accept any and besides, we do not know if they would do it by night or day, and probably some other day.....

You ask if I talk Italian to all these people. Of course I do! B is the only person who talks English. I have been working up my Italian hard recently and can make myself understood and have long conversations, as it is quite easy to understand, and we certainly have plenty of practice.

Bridget clearly though she would have been in a position of command, if only she hadn't been born a woman:-

I am much pleased to hear today that at last they are beginning to fortify a certain position which I have always said would be the weak spot where the Austrians might make a push to get through and they are doing it exactly as I thought it would be necessary. I wonder if my other forecast, which I can't tell you, as you do not know the country, will come off, too.
Oh dear, why couldn't I have been a General!

By the 27th February the Austrian shelling still had not started, probably due to the weather:-

......Yesterday evening we had a spy hunt quite after my own liking. The night of the raid and three succeeding nights we had seen flash signaling not far from here from our window.
Mrs. W---- told one of the Majors and he was much excited, and sent another Captain and Tenente to ask us about it. We went to the farm to see if any flashing was going on, but there was nothing doing. We had, however, marked down the place by certain trees the night before, so they asked us if we would mind guiding them to the place so as to put two Carabinieri on guard. Of course we were only too delighted to go and about five of us started off in the pitch dark and drizzling rain to locate the place. It really was most exciting as the Austrian searchlights were turned on as though they meant to be up to something. Of course we caught no one, but we may still another night. The whole thing was like a Gilbert and Sullivan play. At a given moment, near some cross roads, two Carabinieri in 3-cornered hats and long swords sprang out of a ditch and joined in the hunt.
Speranza, our platone, has to go to Milan to fetch stores soon, and then I shall have to do all the cooking, chopping wood, cleaning, etc.
I can turn out the most delicious meals now, though soldiers' rations don't allow of much variety of menu.

It was all a long way from Little Gaddesden and Cadogan Gardens, where the Talbots had fifteen servants and never had to cook or clean a thing. The world had been turned upside down and Bridget did not seem to mind one bit. However she must have been worried about the risks her younger brother was taking.

On the 12th February, 1916, B wrote in her diary:-
Heard from K(*athleen*) that G(*eoffrey*) had been chasing a German aeroplane and that she had seen it and he was fetching an aeroplane Paris to Dover.

There is an intriguing entry on Friday March 2nd:-

Went to the Villa Bergozzi-nice young cavalry officer who I think invited me to go out riding later but the others were making such a noise singing choruses to comic songs round the piano I cdn't really hear.

Bridget did not seem too upset. However in the archive at Kiplin is a poem it's believed Bridget wrote on a card when in Italy, and brought back with her.

I'm Bridget the fidget

The pride of the canteen

I add up rows of figures

But I don't know what they mean.

My accounts are in a muddle

A fact I don't regret

I've set my cap at Waterfield

And by Jove I'll get him yet.

Sadly, it does not appear as if she did get him. She surely cannot have been short of offers from others, however. Photos of B at this time show a very striking woman, full of sparkle and mischief; so many young men, so few young women, such moments of danger, such a beautiful countryside. A glance at Ernest Hemingway's novel, 'A Farewell to Arms', written as a result of his experiences in Italy in the first world war, reveals some of the passions that flowered in that climate. The hero falls in love with a young English nurse. Did no-one fall in love with Bridget?

Bridget remained in frequent contact with home, receiving letters from Kathleen and a stream of inside information, mainly from Aunt Doobit.

Diary - March 9th Wed, 1916:-
Heard from K that she was thinking of going to La Paume Hosp in Belgium ....
New inventions. Balfour (*former PM and now Foreign Secretary*) had been telling Harry about combined submarine and aeroplane and elastic sides cruiser. Hughie G says that they have had information that the riots in Berlin are very serious and shortage of supplies.

Although Bridget was doing an important job she was well aware that she had no official status and could be moved about at the whim of those in authority. She soon was.

Letter - Monday, March 14th, 1916 :-
My job as field telephonist to the English Hospital has come to an end, as they now belong to a different Army and have to do their transport in another place. It is rather sickening after having done it so long, with very little work, just as the rush begins it should come to an end.
It was quite interesting having to make all the transport arrangements. Last night when I tried to telephone to Cormons for instructions the line had been blown up by a shell.........
The English General, Delme Ratcliffe, was out here today with good news of Verdun, (*where, despite terrible losses, the French*

were holding out) and good news of this fighting, so we feel relieved. Hot sun again, the first since February 25th wonder if this letter will get to England or if the rumour is true that the Germans have broken through and are marching on Paris. *(They had, but were stopped short of the French capital and pushed back.)*

It was not all mud, blood, and bullets. The fighting was taking place in a beautiful part of the country, particularly in spring, and when the fighting paused there was time to luxuriate in it.

Letter - March 17th, 1916:-
It has suddenly turned roasting here — too heavenly.
Yesterday I went up to the hills and basked on a bank of hot smelling thyme in the roasting sun with bees and butterflies buzzing about and gurgling streams all around. Peach and almond trees all pink and the ground one solid mass of primroses, pink and blue bugloss, periwinkles, sweet smelling white and purple violets, anemones, cistus and other things I don't know the name of....
I am illuminating a poem one of the soldiers has written to the King and the Colonel is to present it when he goes past one day.

The pause was brief and the fighting, often hand to hand, soon began again. A frustrated Bridget could only watch from a distance.

We had a thrilling evening a few nights ago watching the battle of Mte San Michele. Shells and shrapnel bursting and the Austrian searchlight bombs. From time to time the big guns stopped and then we knew they were charging.
It is beastly only being a spectator and not being in the thick of it oneself. Telephone messages kept coming in through all the time. 'The Italians have reached the summit'. 'If they can hold on another hour they will have time to dig themselves in'; 'the Austrians are counter attacking' etc. I think our attack was the result of Austrian troops having been withdrawn for Verdun, but

they were hurriedly brought back again. The King and Cadorna went up about 7 and were there all night watching the battle...

Once more there was no Italian breakthrough, the stalemate continued, and normal life resumed.

The Marchese de Reccha came again yesterday from the trenches riding a magnificent charger. He came in just looking like a villain in a comic opera, smacking his boots with his whip and saluting all round... We are longing for a big bath, and not only a small tin of water, and now it is getting hotter the fleas are beginning to hop, skip, and jump. I had a rat in my room last night, and mice are plentiful.

Diary - Monday 20th March 1916:-
I washed my hair-a fearful undertaking as tin pans of hot water had to be brought by Elena down the village street. However it was very successful and my head felt tons lighter.
Heard from K who had been to a play with G, Evelyn and Phyllis Barclay — G supposed to be just off to France again.

Diary - Wednesday 29th March, 1916:-
Geoff had nasty smash when chasing a German but luckily was not badly hurt. His machine crashed into one of the Dover forts and some barbed wire entanglements. He went up next day and Tommies all asked for bits of the smashed propeller which he had to autograph.

In retrospect it would have been better if her brother had broken an arm or a leg so that he would have had to stop flying. The accidents were piling up and Bridget must have known his luck would run out soon, perhaps before she could return to England on leave and see him.

In letters home Bridget was forthright in her political views and she did not think much of H.H. Asquith, the Liberal Prime Minister of the wartime coalition government.

Letter - April 5, 1916:-
Asquith was up this way yesterday, and the Austrian aeroplanes tried to bomb him, but unfortunately failed to do this good service for England and the Allies. I was woken up by 2 or 3 on their way.

This country gets more beautiful every day. All the little round Montega hills covered with white and pink fruit trees and dark cypresses and the fields emerald green, and quantities of purple grape hyacinths and orchids and yellow buttercups. It is extraordinary to see shells bursting behind this sort of background, as they did this morning on San Michele. I have been growing the seeds Aunt D(*oobit-Lady Margaret*) sent me in our garden we have made round the hut today, and wired them in to prevent soldiers tramping on them. They ought to make a lovely mixture if they come up. I have given the rest of the seeds to the hospital. I went into Udine by train yesterday; the first time I had been in a train for three months.

No sooner did I arrive in Udine than there was our old friend the Austrian aeroplane dropping bombs there too.

I am at last getting Lord Monson from Rome and the other Italian committees to send up proper big consignments of sheets, pillows, etc for the hospitals, but there is still a far bigger demand than supply. I have got onto a new Committee in Genoa today, so I hope before the big advance to finish off three or four of the Hospitals with things, but there is a fearful delay on the railways.

Later, April 7th:-
Since writing we have had another air raid last night.
I gather the Italians did not appreciate Asquith much, and would rather have had Lloyd George.
(*LG, a much more dynamic figure, then in charge of military production, would replace Asquith as Prime Minister later that year.*)
We found roses and honeysuckle out yesterday in the hills.
We had a big air attack last night — 13 Austrian machines over at 3 a.m.

We did see one machine brought down quite near by an Italian Ten-Barrachi. We went down to see it this morning and found a large crowd of generals and people inspecting it.

Bridget seems to have been free of hatred for the enemy.

The poor Austrian pilot-quite a young boy — was very badly wounded. They said he was too splendid and refused to answer any questions they asked him.

Perhaps she thought that in another theatre of war it could have been her brother Geoffrey.

In her diary for Thursday 6th May she gave further, more explicit, details. This time she said it was the Austrian observer who......

...was quite splendid quite a boy. He refused to answer any questions although he had one leg severed and the other damaged. The pilot a sergeant also quite young was very pleased to be taken prisoner and said they were tired out from continual flights.

On the 16th April her diary records that she went to the hospital and talked to the Austrian pilot :-

.....a very beautiful boy. One felt quite friendly towards him as he had fallen on his way back from trying to bomb that beast Asquith and so save England.

Bridget gives no indication of her reasons for hating Asquith, who was to lose his eldest son in the war and have another badly injured. He was of course Prime Minister throughout the run up to the war. Did Bridget think the conflict could have been avoided?

There were lighter moments. Bridget's letter of April 7th continued:-

We had two Grenadier Captains to dine last night before they returned to the front line trenches. One brought me a lovely bunch of flowers, carnations, wisteria and lilac....

And she wrote shortly afterwards:-

Did I tell you about the dachshund at San Giovanni, who was run over? The left behind Austrian soldiers gave him a military funeral and hundreds of them followed him to the grave.

It was a brief interlude:-

I have just been dressing a filthy dirty engine driver's badly smashed hand-not a nice job.

And on the 20th April she wrote:-

The tinned meat supplied to the Italian troops from America has had hooks put in by the Germans, and several soldiers have died of eating them.

The next day, Bridget, whose reputation must have spread, was summoned to another frontline makeshift hospital, this time in Cormons, to help with x rays. The hospital had been set up by another of those extraordinary women who, entirely off their own bat, and largely financed by their own money, had decided to set up and run unofficial hospitals just behind the lines.

Letter - Cormons, Easter Sunday, April 22:-

I haven't much time, as Countess Gleichen sent for one of us to come and assist her as the other two people had to return suddenly to England due to illness. It is extraordinarily interesting developing the X ray plates, but one wishes one knew more about it as the smallest mistake may mean a wretched patient having to wait to be done again.

The work was also having to be done in the front line:-

It will be rather difficult developing delicate plates under shell fire, and the Austrians always fire at Red Cross cars. Tomorrow I am going to be taken up in an observation balloon.........

We have had only a few shells here the last few days, but have been warned there may be a big bombardment at anytime, and on Friday the hospitals have been warned to be ready to evacuate if necessary.

I had two very uncomfortable nights here as I had to sleep on a camp bed in the photographic room and the smell of chemicals was not nice, the dust inches thick, lots of mice and rats and one of the windows broken. However, one expects this sort of thing in a war zone.

She wrote in her diary on Monday 25th April 1916:-

Heavy day of developing radiographs — went to Medea and developed in the car with A. Gt success with difficult plate and all the doctors came out and congratulated me and told Gleichen I was a genius etc.

On 30th April she noted in her diary, without comment:-

G(eoffrey) has been chasing German aeroplanes again, in command of War Flight at Dover.

By the middle of May the war seemed to be going badly for the Italians and there was considerable apprehension that the Austrians were about to make a breakthrough. Bridget had moved to nearby Cervignano from where she wrote on the 20th May, 1916:-

Our hospital train didn't get in till late last night, having been delayed 12 hours owing to the rush of trains up North. They are sending up every bit of artillery they can. We have been having a hot time with aeroplane raids lately — on the 14th at midnight 16 bombs all round us, lasting over 2 hours - one man killed and some wounded in a hospital near. Then two nights ago they began coming at 9 and continued to come all night till 4.30, when we saw the last two chased away by an Italian against a brilliant sunrise. The Austrians unfortunately escaped, but the Italian was alas brought down by our own fire...... This place filthy, so there have been many hours scrubbing and spring cleaning everywhere.

Aunt Doobit was proving a faithful correspondent and her letters were full of interesting gossip. Bridget wrote in her diary on Friday 2nd June, 1916 :-

Heard from Aunt D. Prince Xstopher of Greece had been to see her and Mona and just returned from Russia and Berlin.
(*Presumably as Greece was neutral he could travel to both sides*).
He said the Germans were thoroughly sick of the war and really short of food.

And there was bad news of:-

......an awful naval disaster off Jutland — Queen Mary, Black Prince etc all sunk too awful — one can hardly bear to face the Italians after all the admiration they have for our own fleet. I do hope George Pinnock *(a member of her Little Gaddesden scout group in pre war days)* is not on the Black Prince — such a splendid boy and so keen about his job — it wd be terrible if he has gone down. (*He had.*) Heard from H*(umphrey)* and K*(athleen)* that G*(eoffrey)* had gone off to Dunkirk again in command of the War Flight-too disappointing when I hoped to find him in England.

This is the first indication that she hoped to return home on leave shortly. She wrote home on 3rd June:-

The heat is tremendous here now, so please forgive a rather flabby letter. I hope to start back on the 20th, but goodness only knows when I shall arrive, as there is only one small line one can by via Boulogne, and by the 20th that may be blocked too. It looks as though the Italians would manage to hold the Austrians back alright now however so we may not have to escape in a body like Garibaldi.
News of naval fighting in the North Sea just come, only the German version so far. I hope to goodness it is not true we have lost so many ships. *(It was)*

On the 7th June her diary records more bad news:-

Went to Cormons. Terrible news of Kitchener being drowned(*on 5th June 1916 when the warship taking him to meet with the Russians was sunk by a German mine off Scapa Flow*). The It.Newspapers full of admiration and say such a magnificent death on a man of war in a rough sea for the representative of the Great Sea Empire.

There were still pleasant intervals. She wrote home to Kathleen on June 10th about a delightful excursion to an Italian island, undertaken in the middle of a trip to get more supplies for the front:-

.......then to Belvedere, where we had a naval launch and a Tenente waiting to take us to a heavenly little island towards Trieste. It had just a church and the priest's house and the two cottages on it.
The naval commandante and the Tenente had prepared a sumptuous lunch for us. Alpine strawberries, chocolate cakes, champagne etc. The party consisted of two naval officers, the head naval priest, a delightful old brown monk and six of ourselves. Such a comic lot. The monk was such fun. He told Mabel they had been out in a boat the evening before and had been so gay and giddy they couldn't get to sleep and before long the enemy aeroplanes came and dropped bombs and so they had no sleep at all. After lunch the sailors put hammocks up for us under the tree and we rested for an hour. There was a most delicious smell of sea and hay.
Will you be having any leave? (*Presumably she means when she is back home on leave herself*).
This is the last letter we have from this period.

Bridget's diary ends suddenly on the 18th June, 1916.
Eleven days later her brother Geoffrey was killed when his plane crashed in Dover. Bridget was probably already travelling home to meet him when she heard the news. She arrived in time to watch her brother's body being lowered into the ground.

Chapter 4

Kathleen's Early War

Kathleen Talbot was at her sister Bridget's side at the burial of their younger brother. She was the baby of the family, born on the 22nd of November, 1893 and only twenty when war broke out in 1914.

According to a cousin, Barbara Cassell, Kathleen was not very demonstrative, at least in later life, and refused to be called anything other than 'K'.

Mrs.Cassell remembered a close friend of the family, Sir Granville Ram, saying that one could see K deciding she would not be vague and unpunctual like Humphrey and Bridget.

They were ten and nine years older than she was and in their wartime letters to her they sometimes seem to treat her as though she was still a child.

K never went to school, but there was the schoolroom in Little Gaddesden House, and she learned to speak French and Italian, like her sister. She was very musical and had lessons in piano playing, singing, and harmony. The Talbots were a musical family. Geoffrey had started the village brass band in 1902.

Her childhood should have been pretty idyllic with so many grand relatives and so many country houses to visit, but being the youngest of four is not the easiest position to occupy in a family.

She was good friends with Angel (*Angelica Pamela*) Wheatley, who was one of the three daughters of the Ashridge Agent, Colonel Wheatley. He lived in the Elizabethan Manor House in Little Gaddesden. His other daughters were Prudence and Pearl. In 2009, when some floorboards of the Manor House were lifted up, a letter from Angel to K, who was fourteen at the time, was found underneath. Part of it read:

I am so sorry to hear that you are in bed or at least in the house and not able to come out.... I think I shall come to see you this afternoon or tomorrow morning if that will do.
With love
From your loving
Angel

Two years later in 1910 we catch a glimpse of K through the eyes of Conty Talbot *(later Sitwell)*.
Together with her brothers and sister, K was attending a party at the Tea House in the beech woods on the Ashridge Estate. In her book 'Frolic Youth' Conty wrote that:-

Geoffrey had been cooking all day. Ginger, Bridget and K then got up on the top of a large bus *(presumably horse-drawn)*. Angel Wheatley was also a passenger. There were little bunches of flowers –so like the Alfreds.....K had a flashlight photographic apparatus.

When Humphrey and the Geoffrey went off to Imperial India, and Bridget was leading her independent life, turning up and disappearing without warning, K was left at home with her parents.
Before she was out of her teens she had lost both of them, her mother in 1912 and her father the following year. Both died unexpectedly of heart problems. It was a shattering end to childhood.
After their father's funeral K and Bridget stayed on at Little Gaddesden as the children sorted out their parents' financial affairs. There is no record of any disagreements between them about their inheritances.

Soon the sisters were involved in a 'potato venture' and K founded a string band in the village, the precursor of the musical societies and festivals she was to organise in later years. Bridget of course was busy with the local scouts and starting a cooperative gardening scheme.

K still had to be launched into society. At the age of eighteen all upper class girls became debutantes and had to be formally introduced to the aristocratic social scene-and potential husbands. Perhaps, as Kathleen's mother had died when K was eighteen, and she was in mourning, her launch had been delayed. Then the following year her father had also died. So it seems as if she was twenty before her aunt, Lady Brownlow, decided it was time for her first London season. It would be a short one. Even though storm clouds were brewing in June, 1914, few thought that the war was only a few weeks away.

On the 9th of June, 1914, it was reported that, the night before, the Countess Brownlow had held 'a very smart dance' at her home, 8, Carlton House Terrace, for her niece Miss Kathleen Talbot.

'The ballroom was charmingly decorated with festoons of flowers, between which were suspended gold baskets of pink and white pansies'.

The entrance hall was 'full of banks of rhododendrons and white lilies' *(probably from Ashridge)* and the Countess wore 'a gown of cloth of gold and lace'. She welcomed the cream of society including Dukes, Earls, Viscounts, Counts and cabinet ministers, together with the odd Admiral including Prince Louis of Battenberg, who was the cousin of the King and father of the future Lord Mountbatten. Also there were the German Ambassador and his wife. Their embassy was next door at No 9 so it was perhaps simply a courtesy to invite them. There is no record of what Kathleen wore, but presumably she was paraded in glory before potential mates.

And then in August, 1914, the Ambassador and his wife hurriedly packed their bags and left for Berlin, and many of the young men K had met at her coming out ball and in her tour of country houses were answering the call to arms and dying in Flanders fields.

Conty Talbot's new husband Colonel, later General, Sitwell was called back from India and was later to land at Suvla Bay in the disastrous Gallipoli campaign which ended his career and the lives of thousands of British, Australian and New Zealand troops.

The father of a Berkhamsted friend, General Horace Dorrien-Smith of Haresfoot, was soon in action conducting a fighting retreat in Belgium before helping to stabilise the front. Soon the casualties started coming back in convoys to Britain, men without limbs, some blinded, some defaced, some suffering from the effects of mustard gas.

K decided to become a nurse and together with a friend, Millicent Newdigate *(the mother of Barbara Cassell)*, trained as a VAD, a Voluntary Aid Detachment nurse. Angel Wheatley from the Manor House also became a nurse, possibly at Hemel Hempstead. On the 24th May, 1915 K went to nurse at Clopton House just outside Stratford Upon Avon, which had been converted into a hospital, almost certainly because it was run by her aunt, her late mother's sister, Odeyne Hodgson nee De Grey. *(Odeyne was staying in Little Gaddesden House with her sister when she was introduced to the local Vicar, Francis Henry Hodgson, a widower who had three young daughters. There was soon a fourth as Odeyne married the clergyman and a year later had a daughter, Avis Odeyne, who was born in Little Gaddesden. The family had then moved to a living in Escrick, Yorkshire, but by the beginning of the war were in Stratford.)*

The older Odeyne became the Secretary and Commandant of the hospital, which was at first based in the town hall. Her daughter Avis, also became a nurse, and she and Kathleen were soon best friends. As the casualties increased, the hospital expanded to the Hodgsons' home, Clopton House, nearby.

Clopton is an early 17th century country mansion and in 1605 Ambrose Rookwood, one of the Gunpowder Plot conspirators, lived there. Odeyne's father in law had acquired it in 1881.

Nothing in her privileged upbringing could have prepared K for what she saw and had to do.

She was brought up with servants all around, and in the country houses of her relatives every need would have been catered for. Clothes could be left on the floor to be collected and cleaned, evening wear would be carefully laid out, baths would be run and hair would be curled, all by servants who would not have dreamed of having an equal relationship with their masters and mistresses. Now she would be dressing the often evil smelling wounds of those who a few months before might have been her servants, and seeing men naked and in distress. She must have grown up very quickly.

Bridget, dressing wounds in Italy, seems to have been much changed by the experience, regretting the class divisions with which she had been brought up. We have seen nothing to indicate what K's politics were, but she was obviously liked, even loved, by some of those she nursed.

K did not keep any of her own letters from this period, so we have to infer their contents from the replies of her correspondents. As well as the letters from her brothers and sister, she did keep letters from those she had nursed. Some wrote from other hospitals to which they had been transferred, others from their regiments to which they had returned after treatment.

A female colleague called Liddell wrote to K from Clopton when K had taken some leave.
Part of it reads:-

Everybody misses you very much, even Rowan said "I do like Talbot, and am really very sorry she has gone", and Gwyer said with tears in her eyes' "Night duty won't be the same without Talbot"!
The letter ends:-

I miss you very, very much and am counting the minutes until you return. I am perfectly certain you aren't though.

This is probably a reference to the difficult conditions in the hospital outlined elsewhere in the letter.

K and her cousin Avis Hodgson, who was only seventeen when war broke out, were inseparable and they are often mentioned in the same letters. Indeed the friendship continued until Kathleen's death.

K kept up with her ex-patients, sending them letters and photos. On the 12th August, 1915, Rifleman H.Blackley, wrote thanking her:-

......my word we had some fine times there, didn't we? I am so glad the boys are getting on so well, well they cannot help it under all the nurses' kind patient care...

He had a sense of humour.

I like to see chaps work, and I do my hardest to dodge it myself.

On October 27th, 1915, H.Hearne wrote from Epsom Surrey thanking K for a parcel:-

It was very good of you to send it and you can be sure that my tent chums and myself will do justice to the good things it contained. Please thank Nurse Hodgson for the cocoa which will be nice for the cold nights.

In another letter Private Hearne wrote, intriguingly:-

I have missed the milk you used to give me to save me from starvation and should very much like to be ordered to the office after dinner.

There were letters and cards from prisoner of war camps in Germany from British prisoners of war.
Private E.Cooper wrote from Giessen on the 21st November, 1915, thanking K for a 'parcel of eatables' he had received from her via the Red Cross. Future parcels were promised.
(She was also, of course, keeping her brother Geoffrey supplied with plenty of eatables, usually from Fortnum and Mason.)
Another letter from H.Hearne, dated 9th December, 1915, reveals that K was suffering herself:-

I was very sorry to hear from Nurse Hodgson that you had a poisoned arm and hope by now you have quite recovered.

Hearne, though still full of shrapnel in his leg, feared he was about to be sent back to the trenches. He went on:-

I would sooner meet an attack than make one....Your brother *(probably Geoffrey)* was very unlucky to be called back just before Xmas. Unless you have been out there you don't know what a relief it is to get away for a few days.

Some of K's patients did return to the front line, and their penciled notes to her, often poorly spelt, almost all contain the words 'wish I was back at Clopton'.
One in particular, Ginger Norton, tried to meet her in Dover before he went back to France. K was presumably visiting her brother Geoffrey, who was based there with the Royal Navy Air Squadron.
Private Norton wrote:-

....there is not a place like Donty Ward *(at Clopton)*. I will let you know when I get wounded again so you will get me a bed ready will you. I would like to see you before your *(sic)* back. I hope you have a good time while you are hear *(sic)* I do not know of any moor *(sic)* this time only remember me to Nurse Hodgson when you get back.

Ginger Norton was reported missing soon after his return to the front. K kept his letters until she died.

Kathleen must have wondered about the point of bringing these soldiers back to health so that they could be sent back to the front line to be wounded all over again or killed. How emotionally involved with them did she get? She was only twenty one or two at this stage, Avis Hodgson was three years younger and there were clearly bonds of real affection between both cousins and those they nursed. The work must have been not just physically, but also emotionally, exhausting. And then came the news K must have half expected, but been dreading.

Her brother Geoffrey had been the closest of her family to her. While he had been stationed at Dover with the Royal Naval Air Squadron she had been able to visit him and keep him supplied with food and clothing, like the fine warm gloves she bought him. Now he was dead, killed with his mechanic on the 29th June, 1916.

With her parents dying only a few years before, and Bridget and Humphrey overseas, Kathleen had had to manage alone at home. Now, with Geoffrey's death, she had seen half her close family die in less than five years. The war seemed never ending. Who else would die before it was over?

And what was Kathleen to do now? She could hardly remain at home in Little Gaddesden, rattling around in an empty house full of painful memories.

Chapter 5

Bridget's War – Italy

Following her brother's funeral Bridget had decided to return to the Front and by November, 1916, she was back in Italy with Mrs. Watkins.

Italy's Alpine frontier with Austria-Hungary, where Bridget was based, had become, in the words of the historian John Keegan, 'the scene of some of the most extreme fighting of the war'. He describes part of the frontier as a 'howling wilderness' with peaks some six thousand feet high. 'Italian conscripts', Keegan wrote in his book 'The First World War':-

.... 'largely untrained in the demands of mountain warfare, were sacrificed to win narrow slices of harsh upland territory from local (*Austro-Hungarian*) reservists and militiamen who were learning their trade as soldiers in the heat of action.

Neither side had adequate artillery, while the Italians were forced to construct roadways, tactical tracks, cable car railways and precipitous gun positions as they edged their way forward. Troops found shelter in snow tunnels and trenches cut from the rock, and those in the front line of both sides suffering a disproportionate number of head wounds from rock splinters.

The Italian army, in eleven battles of the Alonzo between May 1915 and October 1917, nevertheless succeeded in advancing its front, and defeating an Austrian 'punishment offensive' in the Trentino, although at a terrible cost in lives. .... General Cadorna did his best to increase the number by the ruthless and characteristic institution of the summary execution of stragglers.'

The punishments he inflicted were of a harshness unknown in any of the other armies. Luigi Cadorna, a Northerner who seemed to have contempt for the southern Italian peasants who made up much of his army, believed in summary execution for those who failed to attack and the selection of innocent victims by lot to be shot, following a failed offensive, to encourage the others.

At this stage in her life Bridget was moving towards socialism, believing that the upper classes of Europe had betrayed their peoples. The behaviour of General Cadorna could be seen as evidence of that.

Sometime that year, perhaps as she planned to return to Italy, Bridget compiled a list of what to do and what to take on her journey.

Head washed
Black and white coat,
Overcoat and shirt
Best dark blue or black straw hat
Best brown and best black medium shoes
Riding hat and felt hat
Box for travelling.
Stays
Thermometer
Blue or brown homespun
Dark blue silk and washing cotton voile
Garden hat
Brown suede
Evening gown
Rain wader boots
Cotton voile shirts new

Thus equipped, Bridget returned to her post where, according to Mrs. Watkins, 'Our principal work was feeding and tending to the wounded in trains, administering first aid in our chalet and assisting the Italian Red Cross Doctor in the station'.
Also in the area, at the Villa Zucco in Cormons, was Unit 4, the radiographic unit run by Lady Helena Gleichen and Mrs. Nina

Hollings who had raised the money to pay for the equipment they operated. Lady Helena was a painter of landscapes, flowers and animals, with a particular passion for horses. Her sister was a sculptor. They were the children of a half nephew of Queen Victoria. During World War One, Lady Helena renounced her German titles and accepted the rank of a Marquess's daughter. As we have seen, Bridget had helped them out on occasions and would do so again.

The first of Bridget's letters to have survived from the period after Geoffrey's death is from the small town of Cervignano just south of Udine, a railhead a few miles from the front and just north of the Adriatic coastline:-

Cervignano
Nov 25 1916 c/o Captain Spencer
2 Whitehall Court
S. W.

Dear K

So far I have not has a single letter or wire since I arrived here. We are so cut off from Udine one doesn't get them. I am hoping a motor cyclist may be going in today possibly. I sent you a birthday wire but I do not suppose it had arrived and asked for a wire to be sent about Aunty A (*Adelaide, Lady Brownlow, who was seriously ill*)

I am getting into touch with the Field ambulances and hospitals up on this front now as this is where the fighting will be more now. The Austrians made a sharp attack on Montfalcone two days ago to celebrate Franz Josef's death and we are to attack again soon now. Duino is the next big bit we have to take to the N of Trieste and they have to work round it. I very much doubt their taking Duino before the spring — our Austrian landlady who has been interned for a year has now returned and tried to suffocate an Italian nurse in the Course by smoking her room at 3 in the morning. She just managed to stagger to the window but nearly died of it since! The Austrian needless to say is still there so we shall probably be knifed or something.

Gleichen and Hollings have both been recommended for the Blue Valour medal which fills us with envy —we may get the ordinary war medal perhaps. There is a gt.plague of rats in the trenches and lots here. They drink all the ink and eat the metal of the bottles in the Casa del Soldato. Teresa has had a bomb through their house in Venice right from top to bottom.

A half English boy came in two days ago after a hot time taking up ammunition. He had to take 11 mortars and did not know the way and the guide ran away. A shell caught one mortar and set it on fire and exploded all the ammunition and then it caught on the next and as they were on the edge of a precipice they didn't turn round so they had to push the other mortars round and unload them as fast as they could under very heavy fire.

Yr letters and others just come. I am so glad you can get over to Belton (*where Countess Adelaide was being treated*) for a few days and how very nice going on a first class pass — what swank.

The next letter is to her brother Humphrey Talbot, training in England with the Army Service Corps. before going to the Western Front, where the fighting was grinding millions into the earth.
She must have feared for her remaining brother's life but of course could not say so.
If she did not have it already, she now demonstrates an air of command, particularly in the postscript. She clearly thought that if a Talbot spoke, others would listen.

Nov 30 1916 Posto di Ristoro Inglese
Cervignano
Dear Humph ...Quite a rush of work here which is a good thing as I don't think Gleichen is going to take me on at present. She had Ethel Smythe the opera writer out here and she scandalised the Italians by strutting up and down Goritzia with an eyeglass and a cigarette! I wish I cld tell you a most dramatic tale of 2 foreign staff officers but must wait till I get back - we went to Aquilia yesterday after the train and saw a new bit of Roman mosaic pavement the priest Don Constantino had been finding yesterday. It was very nice to be the first people to see it for 1500 years. It

was a most perfect bit of design with a big lobster and different sorts of birds and a donkey — brilliant colouring.

The latest crime of the old Austrian landlady here is to pull down our dugout. She is an awful old woman and has been interned for a year so I can't think why she is let loose now.

Much love to all

Yr lovin.

Bridget GT

(*written across letter*)

If you have time I wish you wld go or telephone the Headquarters of the YMCA and ask them if something can be done to get a club started for our sailors at Taranto. The present YMCA is too far from the docks to be any use and it is too wretched for them to have nowhere to go to. Ask them to write to me and tell me the conditions.

Two weeks after this letter, on 13th December 1916, known as 'White Friday', ten thousand soldiers were killed by avalanches in the Dolomites just above where Bridget was based.

Chapter 6

Kathleen's War - England

Within a couple of weeks of her brother Geoffrey's death Kathleen Talbot had decided to go back to nursing. What was the alternative? Bridget was going back to Italy, and Humphrey was preparing to go to France. It would have been unbearably lonely to have stayed in a deserted Little Gaddesden House, surrounded only by ghosts and memories.

On the 9th July 1916, she had another letter from Hall's Croft, Stratford-Upon-Avon, again probably from her aunt Odeyne, Commandant of Clopton Hospital:-

Dearest K, it is splendid of you to come back to Clopton. I expect you will find life easier while you are working, but the effort to begin anything again must be dreadful. <u>Don't</u> come til you know the Convoy is here. I have been up at Clopton doing quartermaster this week. One does miss you dreadfully there.

So a sorrowing Kathleen went back to Clopton, though she often thought of going to nurse in France or Belgium, or better still go to be with Bridget in Italy where they had spent happy holidays in those far off pre-war days.
That Christmas her Uncle Reggie wrote to her from 12, Manchester Square, London:-

Margaret and I send our best wishes for 1917 and hope that it may be full of happiness for you dearest girl and bring all sorts of good things.
1916 has been a horrible year.... With heart felt wishes for a Happy New Year and peace after victory.
Love to Odeyne.
Reggie.

Peace after victory was nowhere in sight, millions more were to die, and the convoys of the injured kept arriving at Clopton. K was back in the old exhausting routine, nursing, sending food parcels to prisoners of war, looking after the family home in Little Gaddesden and then acting as secretary to her surviving brother, Humphrey, as well as keeping him supplied with the best Fortnum and Mason had available. She was also writing to former patients who had left Clopton and were now returned to their regiments.

Private McLean wrote to Nurse Talbot in February thanking her for some photos, remembering 'happy times at Clopton' and saying that 'my leg is doing fine — kindly remember me to all the nurses'.

Later that month K was able to have a few days holiday with Avis. Then, on March 15th, 1917, Sergeant H.Cass, alias Suffering Anthony, wrote to K from nearby Hill House Hospital in Warwick to say that

'I had my shoulder reopened, and it has now nearly reached the stage of when you had to deal with it.' His foot was also giving him trouble....

'Personally I think that what with my hands, foot, thigh and back, they didn't pay much attention to my ankle'.

He spoke of the 'many kindnesses' he had received at Clopton, and went on... 'Clifford is President of the Revolutionists here, only last night we held a meeting and decided to burn Warwick. Should the Revolution spread to Clopton, we will take into consideration all you nurses done for us when we were helpless'. K must have been reassured.

It isn't clear whether Suffering Anthony is joking or not, though he may well have been. Of course in early 1917 revolts had started to break out among the armed forces in Russia and later that year the Communists took over the Government there. The British establishment was very worried that revolution could break out in Britain.

The day after that letter was written news came of another death very close to home. On March 16th, 1917 the Countess Brownlow,

Aunt Addy, died at Belton. Though she had been ill for some time the news must have been a considerable blow to K who, like just about everyone who knew her, admired and loved the Countess. However, many aristocratic contemporaries thought her over susceptible to the feelings of others and too vulnerable to their distress. Her brother-in-law Lord Pembroke said 'Poor little Adelaide has got such a terrible loving heart that life must always be more pain than joy to her'.

K's cousin Conty *(Talbot)* Sitwell described Lady Brownlow this way:-

When one looks back and thinks of all the servants.., it seems queer that we should have taken so much for granted, a magnificence which appears feudal-almost royal-now, and it is difficult to give an impression of such a mode of living, and of the earnest and humble Christianity which accompanied it day by day, without laying it open to the charge of insincerity.., or careless ease. Yet ease there was not in the presence of Adelaide Brownlow... her whole being was bent on helping others... how often the half-eaten ham had disappeared and was found to have accompanied her on the afternoon drive, and been left at a lonely cottage. 'Adelaide, you will leave me some of that ham won't you, before you run away with it?' I remember Cousin Addie saying, with his loud laugh, after cutting off a slice for himself.... At her funeral the tear-stained faces of the cottage women were there in scores.

K was present at the funeral which took place at Belton church on Wednesday, March 21st, 1917 at 1 pm.

On the front of the Order of Service was this quotation, 'God is Love, and he that dwelleth in love, dwelleth in God, and God in him'. A 16th Century Prayer was read 'O Lord, support us all the day long of this troubled life, until the shades lengthen and the evening comes, and the busy world is hushed, the fever of life is over, and our work is done. Then, Lord, in Thy Mercy, grant us safe lodging, a holy rest, and peace at the last, through Jesus Christ our Lord. Amen'. At the graveside Psalm 23- 'The Lord is my Shepherd' was read. On the far side of Belton Park from the Church the Machine Corps temporarily suspended their target practice. Afterwards the grieving Adelbert erected a cross on the Green at Little Gaddesden. It was placed outside the Manor House and is also visible from the main entrance of Ashridge House. Around its base the Earl had inscribed these words.

In Remembrance
Of
Adelaide
Wife of Adelbert
3rd Earl Brownlow
Born 1844
Married 1869
Died 1917
Daughter of
Henry 19th Earl of
Shrewsbury and Talbot

Mercy and Truth have met together
Righteousness and Peace have kissed each other

Humphrey was unable to get leave to come back from Flanders for the funeral but Bridget had returned from Rome and wrote to H that she was 'remaining at Belton for some time'. Doubtless she was helping to comfort Uncle Addy and sort out her aunt's estate. The Earl seems to have been in a state of collapse and his nephew and nieces were very worried that he would not recover. Ashridge remained shut up and Lord Brownlow rarely left Belton until his death in 1921.

Chapter 7

Humphrey's
War - France

The first letter we have from Humphrey to his sister Kathleen is dated two months before the death of his aunt, Jan 22, 1917. He was about to embark for France. He was thirty three and a lieutenant in the Army Service Corps. and it appears that he had only just finished his training. He had come late to the war. Why?

Until the Military Service Bill was introduced in January, 1916, Britain's army had been a voluntary one. After that date all men between eighteen and forty one were liable to be called up. Conscription had been unthinkable in 1914. After all, the war was going to be over by Christmas, there was no shortage of volunteers, and young men were encouraged to go by appeals to their sense of duty, and by the suggestion that if they didn't they would be short of female company. Marie Lloyd, the Queen of the Music Hall, and of sexual innuendo, sang popular songs like, 'I didn't like you much before you joined the army, John, but I do like you, cockie, now you've got your khaki on'. All the nice girls might love a sailor, but the naughty ones seemed more likely to fall for men with moustaches in army uniform.

By 1916, however, it was clear the war was not going to be over soon and that the Allies might even be defeated. There was as yet no sign of the United States entering the conflict, Britain's casualties were mounting, and there were real worries that the French armies, which had suffered even worse losses, might crack. There was another, rather embarrassing, reason for conscription. Around thirty per cent of British males were not fit enough to fight. The pool of available men was shrinking alarmingly.

Why had Humphrey not volunteered, in 1914? It seems that he was working on the East Indian Railways at the onset of war in charge of traffic, and, since his younger brother, Geoffrey, seemed mustard keen to join up and fly aircraft, perhaps it was thought one brother at risk was enough. Also Humphrey was for some years a possible heir to his grandfather the Earl of Shrewsbury, his father's elder brothers not having had sons. Perhaps Humphrey waited in India to see how the war went and whether it would be over quickly. However, when conscription was introduced in January 1916, and after the death of his brother Geoffrey later that year, Humphrey must have felt he had to join up. After all he was a Talbot, with an Admiral and one of Britain's most admired Generals for uncles. He does not, however, seem to have been a natural warrior.

Humphrey John Talbot was born on the 8th October 1883 at Little Gaddesden House in Hertfordshire, the first child of Alfred and his wife, the former Emily Augusta Louisa De Grey.

He should have had an idyllic childhood. The British Empire was at its zenith and Humphrey had been born near the zenith of its ruling establishment. His family had a house in fashionable Chelsea, and he sometimes stayed at the Brownlow's magnificent London home, next to St James's Park. He spent weekends at country houses all over Britain and particularly enjoyed going to his Uncle Brownlow's shooting lodge by Loch Canisp in the Highlands of Scotland, or North Britain as he would have called it.

Yet it seems there was something awkward about Humphrey. He was never quite at ease, seemed more comfortable in the company of older people, and was wary of change. He appeared to be more at home in the past than the present. According to a relative, Barbara Cassell, Humphrey was also prey to long periods of depression, particularly in his later life.

Humphrey, H to his family, was educated first at home and then at Evelyns School at Colham Green, near Uxbridge. The school had been founded in 1872 and maintained close relations with Eton, to where H duly went. He was in H.E Luxmoor's House. He went on to Christ Church Oxford, took his degree, and then had to decide on a career. Although they had very rich connections, and plenty of stately homes to visit, the Alfred Talbots do not seem to have had a lot of ready cash, so H would have to get a job. Fortunately one of his uncles came up trumps.

Major General the Hon. Sir Reginald Arthur James Talbot KCB CB was coming to the end of a glorious military career and had just finished commanding the Army of Occupation in Egypt.

Somehow or other he had found the time to be an ADC to the Queen, become MP for Stafford at the age of twenty eight, pose for 'Spy' and several fashionable painters, and marry Margaret Stuart-Wortley, who became Aunt Doobit to her doting nephews and nieces. In 1904 he became Governor of Victoria in Australia, and invited H, aged twenty one, to be his assistant private secretary. The Reginald Talbots stayed in Melbourne for four years and both were widely admired. This period as private secretary to a very successful Governor ought to have been an ideal launching pad for Humphrey. Surely the Foreign Office or Diplomatic Service or Parliament should have been open to him? Nothing substantial seems to have resulted.

We catch occasional glimpses of him at Little Gaddesden. He was treasurer of the local scout group, founded by his much more dynamic sister, Bridget. One of his cousins Conty Talbot *(later Sitwell)* refers to him in her book of memoirs 'Frolic Youth'. In 1909, when H was just twenty six, Conty calls him 'Old Ginger', presumably there was a younger one as well, but it also suggests perhaps that he was prematurely middle aged and somewhat set in his ways. Conty, a natural rebel, mentions an earnest H trying to persuade her to be a Conservative. He was unsuccessful, but she was clearly fond of Humphrey. In August 1910 she went to Ashridge, where H was treated almost as a son. 'Old Ginger came quickly to the door to greet me. I was glad to see him. He is always the same'.

At Christmas 1910 Conty's family home, Marchmont, Water End near Hemel Hempstead-now a pub — The Marchmont

Arms - was full of Talbots and Custs. Harry Cust, the notorious ladies' man, was also present. He was believed to have fathered numerous children by other men's wives. Lady Diana Cooper said he was her real father. He was regarded as a great wit, edited the Pall Mall Gazette and was the heir to childless Lord Brownlow. Unfortunately for him he died a few months before the Earl he had waited so long to succeed.

Conty wrote of that evening, 'Ginger was so lively that Harry *(Cust)* said "Humphrey is not himself tonight: something must be done".'

It is hard to resist the thought that H had become a figure of fun; serious, earnest, a worrier, with little small talk and not quick at the sort of repartee which Conty loved. Nonetheless he did take part in the Christmas theatricals that year.

Within four years all had changed utterly. Humphrey's mother and father had died and he had become head of the family, trying to sort out all the family finances, while still working for the East India Railways. Then war had been declared, the blinds had come down on Ashridge and Belton, the army had moved in, and Bridget, Geoffrey and Kathleen had gone off to war. All Humphrey loved was now under threat.

'The lights had gone out all over Europe' and, one is tempted to think, in H's own life.

Then in 1916 his brother's luck had run out. Geoffrey Talbot had been in so many plane crashes, and walked away relatively unharmed, that perhaps it seemed that the inevitable might be postponed indefinitely. It could not be. At Dover, on a blustery day, Geoffrey died shortly after take off. Now Humphrey, nearly thirty three, would have to join up, but join what?

H was not short of influential connections, not least his still active Uncle Reggie who sometimes had his old colleague, the Secretary for War, Lord Kitchener at his dinner table, yet Humphrey ended up in the unglamorous Army Service Corps. This is how it is described by Dr David Payne, in his article 'The British Army

Service Corps On The Western Front In The Great War' for the Western Front Association:-

The ASC was one of the Cinderella units of the Western Front and it received little in the way of commendation, or entries, in the official reports of the Great War. Although the two hundred thousand plus officers and men of the ASC who served on the Western Front could not normally be considered combat soldiers, many were exposed daily to the capricious dangers of the battlefield as they moved around it performing their varied duties of supplying and transporting the fighting man. Certainly the German artillery deliberately concentrated on the ASC supply routes, depots and resting places of the ASC's animals of burden.

On occasion, when the military situation demanded (e.g. The German Spring Offensive, March 1918) the ASC troops were ordered to take up their rifles and were drafted into the Front-line defences. Also, whole groups of ASC men were drafted into Front-line battalions and other active service units as replacements for casualties while their place was taken by troops who were not considered fit enough for Front-line duty i.e. 'B' and 'C' medically graded ASC men. Something like a total 100,000 fit ASC troops were so released and retrained for posting to fighting units on the Western Front, including over 100 officers to the Royal Flying Corps. The varied dangers faced by ASC troops are attested to by their overall casualty rates that totalled 160,000 (4.9%) with 22,600 (0.8%) killed in action, or died of wounds. Another 5,900 died of disease (1.8%).

Everything that the soldier needed at the front, guns, ammunition, food, clothing, had to be transported there by the ASC, often under fire. It required immense courage to fight in the front line, but it required no little courage to keep on returning there, albeit for short periods, and after some days back behind the lines in rather less danger. Presumably it was Humphrey's experience of helping run the East Indian Railways which was a decisive factor in his deployment.

Dr David Payne again:-

To move the huge quantities of materials that were required to fight the War, the ASC relied extensively on the existing national railways and waterways in the UK, France and Belgium. In addition, the Royal Engineers built an extensive network of small gauge railways to connect the railheads in France and Belgium with the Front Line and so greatly facilitated the working of the ASC supply chain and the movement of heavy artillery and tanks.

Someone who had already extensive experience of running railways would be useful.

The following letters were mainly sent from Humphrey to his sister Kathleen, or K, who was nursing near Stratford on Avon. Her eldest sister Bridget was, of course, with Mrs. Watkins on the Italian Front.
The letters begin in January, 1917 when Lieutenant Humphrey Talbot, thirty three, having finished his training and having had his official photograph taken by someone called Beresford, is about to depart for France and the Western Front. Although obviously caring a great deal for his younger sister he does sometimes seem to be treating her as his secretary, even though she is a full time nurse:-

January 22, 1917 A.S.C. Mess, Bulford Camp, Salisbury (from joint H/c)
Beresford has not sent the proofs yet
Dear K.
Will you please pay the enclosed unless it is some order of yours or Bridget's. The newspaper account for the year usually comes from Smith's London office and I think I have had some Bradshaws and other papers beside Punch. Bridget wrote dated January 12 to say that things were getting very slack at Cervignano and that she expects soon to be making tracks for England.
I have had another busy day today going over to Tidworth to draw stores this mng and practising my section on convoy duty this af/n. The roads are like glass which adds to the excitement.

We had one collision and one lorry nearly upset but eventually got all safe back to the Square. Probably we shall be off in a few days now. Yr loving H Talbot

Sunday 28th Jan, 1917 A.S.C. Mess Bulford Camp Salisbury
Dear K
Here are the photographs (*of Humphrey in uniform*) from Beresford for your approval. I have marked the 1st 3. X which I think is the best.
Will you please order a dozen or so mixed from these or any others you like and send Beresford a cheque for 30/- on my behalf When signing Coutts cheques you had better show in some way that you are writing for me - such as a/c H.J Talbot otherwise Mr. Coutts might get mixed up as I continue to draw cheques myself
We are off tomorrow going to Codford to pick up Guns and artillery stores. Sleep there Monday night, Tuesday night at Wickham,Wednesday at Portsmouth. Vehicles and personnel there separate I believe, one or other sailing from Southampton.
But I haven't got orders yet on this point and we might be a day or two before sailing if the docks are congested. I wonder if the National Service Scheme will remove all the male staff from Gaddesden. If so old Boarder will have to carry on single handed as best he can. I have had a nice job getting everything ready especially in this horrible cold. Half the men sick or absent — my second officer quite nice but very young.
Yr loving
HT
(*attached is a newspaper cutting which says 'The undermentioned temp 21K1 Lts to be temp Lts and to retain their actg. Rank where specified'. The names include H J Talbot*)

Subsequent letters are full of instructions for bills Humphrey wanted K to pay. We have deleted most of them.

Feby 1st 1917 Thursday night George Hotel Portsmouth

(The notepaper is stamped with the following —
Sept 14th 1805. It was here Lord Nelson spent his last hours
in England)

Dear K.

I am really at the Clarence Barracks, but it is easier to write here. We left Bulford on Monday night with our convoy and got to Codford via Stonehenge at about midday. There we picked up the 6th Howitzers and stayed the night. The Fanes (Hon. Trefusis) were away from Boyton so Crawford and I billeted ourselves in a house close by and were very comfortable. Tuesday we had a long run towing the guns to Wickham going via Salisbury and Romsey. At Wickham we were very lucky and stayed for the night with Sir Robt and Lady Lowry. He was in command at Rosyth at the beginning of the war. A regular jolly sailor and a gt friend of Charlie Beresford's. Yesty we have moved on here via Fareham and Cosham and are now waiting for embarkation orders. We may go soon or wait some days according to how the transports come in. I shall probably sail with the men from Southampton and my 21K1 officer will take the vehicles from here. The barracks are really at Southsea, but Portsmouth and Southsea are all close together.

It is still very cold and it has been trying to snow — Pinnock who brought some last things for me to Wilton, reported snow and very cold at Gaddesden.

I handed him over to Challis and hope he saw something of Wilton garden .... This is one of the Public House Trust homes and is under the same control as the Bridgewater Arms *(in Little Gaddesden)*.

Quite nice and clean and somewhere to know of in such a dirty town. I telephoned to Aunty D last night but she was in bed with rheumatism and Winny answered for her!.

Have you heard any more of B's plans — I sent her a wire today saying I was here awaiting orders.

Now I must run off and see the Adjutant who is an old Grove Park acquaintance. Will let you know my future addresses.

Yr loving

H Talbot

The next day Humphrey finally embarked for France and the Front. A few weeks after he arrived Lady Brownlow died. There was no question of H getting leave for the funeral, so soon after arriving.

BEF France
Monday 5th march 1917
Dear K.,
I hope you will have got some news of me by now as I have written to most of the family since I arrived at this 'somewhere' village.
Today thick snow again but it is rapidly melting and turning into delicious mud. Traffic is rather held up in consequence.
I am glad that Pinnock is devoting his energies to growing vegetables in the flower beds..... Strand magazine for March quite interesting. Heard from B. in Rome where she seems to be enjoying herself. She doesn't say if she is returning home, but rather sounds as if she meant to return to Cervignano for a bit. Many Thanks for jam and potted pheasant from F And M if you were the sender. Goodnight.

Your loving H Talbot

BEF France
Friday March 23rd 1917 8am
(in pencil)
Dear K,
Thanks for various letters received. I have been out for five consecutive days and nights with a few hours sleep thrown in so I am fairly tired and haven't had much time to write. As fast as the lorries come in from one job they are turned round and sent off on another. We got in at 5.45am this morning and the unfortunate men are waiting to go off again straight away. There are 75 lorries standing in the street ready to go off. The Germans ought to have a dose of shells presently judging by the number we have moved lately. Our guns have shifted to another position for a short time. It was a long job moving them, the Germans have been shelling some of the other batteries and the road was full of pits in consequence. I do wish I could get home to help Uncle Addy at this time. Is he keeping all right? It seems so difficult to imagine things going on

without dear Auntie Addy as everything seemed to centre round her and she was so much the mainspring of the family.

I wonder where she is to be buried at Belton — whether in or outside the Church? I hope Pinnock produced some nice flowers — Perhaps it is all for the best that she should have died now and not had a long illness as one knows what a trial it would have been to her not to be able to be up and doing. Do write and tell me all that is going on. Is Aunt D having a good rest?

Very cold again and snow here - Too sleepy for more now.

Your Loving,

Humphrey

Much love to Uncle Addy and I hope to write soon

Hughie has asked me to be godfather to 'Gustavus Adolphus'.

H wrote again the next day obviously upset that he could not get back to help his uncle and the rest of the family:-

BEF France

Saturday March 24th 1917

Dear K

I wish I could be home now to help generally, but we are kept working full time as things are likely to be busy — I have been out 5 nights and days this week and all but got sent off on a long expedition this morning.

I am afraid Uncle Addy will be dreadfully lonely but we must all try to cheer him up — B says she is remaining at Belton for some time.

Yr Loving H.Talbot

We change to summer time tonight. That is 11pm becomes M.N.

BEF France

Saturday March 31 1917

Dear K.,

Thanks for the 3 letters which I haven't had a chance of answering before. I have only had 2 nights in bed since the 18th so you can imagine we have been fairly busy. Thousands of shells have gone up to the batteries. There may be a push soon in this district but one hears so many rumours. My address is slightly altered and should now read ASC 252 SBAC A Siege Park 1 Corps BEF France.

Humphrey had decided to sell the Talbots' London home in Cadogan Gardens. After all, who was there to live in it?

.......I am carrying on negotiations with Trollope about possibly selling 28 CG. There is a man who seems rather keen but of course I must wait and see what he is prepared to offer. He would want to take possession at Midsummer. It is difficult to know what is the best thing to do, but we so seldom get any use out of the house that I really think a flat or a smaller house would suit us very much better.

I wonder what we can invent to interest Uncle Addy.? Couldn't he do something in connection with the forestry schemes they have been suggesting in the newspapers. Perhaps he could make a motor expedition to Virginia Water *(near Windsor)* to see the Canadian lumber camp there. I went there one day from Fulham. Or he would find a trip out here very interesting and he could probably manage to see all that is possible.

The Boche has been more lively lately round here and has been shelling several of the villages we pass through and also dropping shells near our battery.

War held little attraction for Humphrey and after only a few months service he was longing for its end:-

I wish the beastly war would get on and get finished, but it seems likely to go on for ages yet and probably starvation all round will end it rather than actual fighting. I don't know what to advise you as to your own plans but I should think you would be glad to be in England for a bit after being away so much. (*Has he confused her with Bridget?*) I expect there will probably be some forms for me to sign in connection with Probate, but I expect Uncle A's lawyers will send on anything which is necessary.

Post time. Much love to all and let me know what is happening.

Yr Loving

H Talbot

BEF France
April 11th 1917
Dear K.
Will you deal with the enclosed from the Household a/c. Do you think it extravagant to keep feeding the doves *(at Little Gaddesden)* in wartime.? I take it this includes pigeon food as well.

I suppose you have seen all the details of the last most successful advance and the huge numbers of Boche prisoners taken. Another 2,000 yesterday in addition to the 11,000 already mentioned. We passed hundreds of them on the road yesterday afternoon. Mostly old or quite young and no middle aged. They didn't look the least starved but very glad to be prisoners.

The weather continues vile. Snow yesterday and more rain today. No other news. Yr loving

Humphrey Talbot

The Harrods Bill I asked you about has turned up

BEF France
Thursday 12th April 1917
Dear K
I wish we could find a new tenant for 28 CG for the summer, it was sad the proposed sale not coming off.

Weather here still perfectly beastly. I was out all last night in a raging blizzard. Snow drifts in places 4 ft deep and the lorries in all sorts of difficulties. Even the rescuing caterpillar got frozen up!

I had a line from Nannie who says she is much better but she has not been downstairs yet (April 7th)

We passed lots more Hun prisoners this morning. A villainous looking crowd. No other news and much too sleepy to write any more.

Yr Loving

H Talbot

Did you pay Automobile Association subscription? If not please do so from joint a/c I think it is worth continuing even though we are not using a motor

BEF France
Thursday 19th April 1917
Dear K.

Two letters dated 12th and 14th inst also Punch and Bystander arrived this evening for which many thanks.

Your letter about letting 28CG dated 13th arrived yesterday. I think almost I had better accept Best and Gapp's offer of 10 guineas for 3 months from May 4th. The house ought to fetch more but there has been no other offer and it is a great thing to get it off one's hands. Probably directly I settle a better offer will come along which is what always happens. I will communicate direct with the Agent.

You ought not to pay me anything for the Potato Venture as it was entirely you and B's idea with G Bunn as manager.

Are you doing anything about renewing the Petrol Licence which I think expires this month? The papers say no more petrol is allowed to private owners unless the car is used for work of National importance so perhaps we can't get any. G Bunn has the licence, but probably has not bought all the petrol it entitles us to as the motor hasn't been out. This won't make any difference though as you can only get a certain amount each month and you cannot accumulate your allowance.

The weather still wet and beastly but in spite of it both we and the French seem doing very well and taking any amount of prisoners and guns. Crawford is away for 2 or 3 days moving a gun so I am alone pro tem. Now to bed and so goodnight,
Yr Loving HTalbot

BEF France
25th April 1917
Dear K

Here is a notice about petrol for the motor which is sad, but it was only what I expected after seeing the papers. If only some of what is wasted daily out here cd be saved there wd be plenty to go round. I wrote to G.Bunn and told him to buy all the petrol he was entitled to under our expiring licence so that the motor cd be used in any gt emergency. Otherwise we shall have to fall back on Kitty *(their horse)* or flys *(horse drawn carriages)* from Meek. I am feeling pretty annoyed as they are taking away Crawford (my 2' officer) also one of my sergeants and a corporal! It is some sort of plot so that they can keep another officer and 2 NCO's at HQ

They are always playing dirty tricks on one and it certainly is a thankless task to run a column. I wish they wd hurry up and finish the war. There seems to be tremendous fighting going on by the news in the communiqués. We haven't been quite so busy lately though there has been pretty constant work. There was a most thrilling air fight over here yesterday and they say the Taube was brought down.

Our men were pressing him hard when we last saw them.

Much love. Yr loving H.Talbot

BEF France
25. 4. 17
Dear K

Your letter of the 20th arrived tonight after I had already written to you. It wd be very nice if you cd manage to get out here and be somewhere near. (*K had begun to apply to work as a nurse in a hospital in France or Belgium*) There are plenty of Casualty Clearing Stations about and a hospital on the new approved lines in a villager about 2 miles away.

I think B would do well to undertake Mrs W's scheme *(back in Italy)* if Uncle Addy doesn't want her. Why shouldn't she persuade him to go out too?

Goodnight Yr Loving

Humphrey Talbot.

I was so sorry to hear about poor Claudie Bertie (*Captain Claude Peregrine Bertie of the Royal Flying Corps had been killed in action aged 26 on the 19th March. His death had only just been announced*)

Bridget did indeed return to Italy, and Uncle Addy remained in mourning at Belton, but what had Kathleen decided to do?

Chapter 8

Kathleen – Staff Nurse Talbot

After the funeral of her aunt at Belton in March 1917, K went back to Clopton where a few days later she received a letter from a former colleague called Betty Lash, who was now at the Military Hospital, Fargo, on Salisbury Plain. K had evidently been promoted.

Dear 'Staff Nurse' Talbot!
You will think I have forgotten you as I have not written before now, but it is not likely, you are one of the last I shall forget at Clopton for many reasons and one of them is the great help you were to me the weeks that followed our last July Convoy. What I should have done without you and Poole I know not, we got through some work.
I received a letter from N. Hodgson, or ought I to say Theatre N Hodgson, this morning. It amused me highly and I am still laughing! Let me congratulate you both on your promotion and may I take some of the credit on myself as having been responsible for <u>some</u> of your past training. I am not meaning to sound sarcastic, really. I am more than glad that you are both capable of so much.

As her brother Humphrey, behind the lines on the Western Front, did not express such confidence in K's ability to handle his various cheque books and pay the family bills, this must have been a welcome boost to the youngest Talbot's confidence.
Despite her promotion it is difficult not to feel sorry for Kathleen at this point. She was just twenty four, had suffered from a poisoned wrist, was working flat out at Clopton, had just lost a much loved aunt, was trying to arrange for her bereaved uncle to go on holiday, was also conducting a joint Potato Venture with

Bridget, was trying to sell the house in St Anne's Buildings, Westminster, which she had inherited from her parents, and was handling all the family accounts while her two elder siblings were out of the country. And then she was told off by her slightly tetchy older brother for confusing bank accounts.

However she had some more good news on June 16th, Uncle Addy, writing from Belton House on black edged paper, told K that he was sending her one of Adelaide's rings. It was the 'Cabachon Sapphire and Diamond Ring'.

He also said, "I am very much interested in the house at Holy Isle, and would certainly try to pay you a visit there, and look forward to it with delight".

K began to plan for their summer holiday in Northumberland.

Chapter 9

Bridget – The English Canteen

After spending some time with her grieving Uncle Addy at Belton, Bridget had once more returned to the Italian Front, where Italian forces had still not made a breakthrough, despite appalling casualties. Their morale was poor and there were rumours of another enemy offensive. The next letter from B which has survived is to Uncle Reggie's wife, Margaret, better known as Aunt Doobit. With no children of her own, she took a particular interest in her nephews and nieces, and seems to have an open door policy at her home in central London. (*However that home was in danger of being bombed as the German Zeppelin raids got underway. Britain was no longer an island when it came to warfare.*)

Not only was Aunt D kind and concerned, as we have already noted she was also excellently connected to the political and military establishments, mainly through her husband the Major General. Their Manchester Square home in London's West End was also perfectly situated for dinner parties with the powerful into whose ears words from the Fronts could be dropped.

On June 7, 1917, Bridget wrote to her. The military position on the Italian front was clearly deteriorating which, paradoxically, made B feel more exhilarated:-

Address English Canteen *(page corner torn)*
Headquarters
Commando Ragguppamento B
Xl Corpo d'Armata
Zona di Guerra
Italy
Dear Aunt D
You must forgive this untidy scrap this time as our luggage has not come yet and we are living in real war conditions. Such a journey

fearfully hot and long and then a most alarming interview in Turin with Gen H(amilton) at a villa outside. (*Was this about the deteriorating situation at the front?*).

Gen H and Col Gabriel came on our train up to the front where we found conditions v much changed. Mrs Watkins back but not v strong. The house opposite ours was hit and she saw it go down like a pack of cards and 23 people were buried under it — too awful. They managed to get 18 out alive. The hospital (in whose grounds is our hut) is only P.A.M.C. no nurses please tell K (*who had also thought of moving to Italy to nurse*) and is being moved back a mile or so next week which is sad as the wounded. Tommies are so nice and excited over the canteen opening and say they have been longing for it for ages. (*Some British troops had been moved to the Italian Front to support the hard pressed General Cardona*) Gen H is very keen about it which is a good thing and goes into every detail about stores prices etc and has made out a list of regulations for us we are not allowed to go and dine in any mess or go in any motor unless they bombard and then we are to go at once! They don't think they will again now the hospital is being moved Things have not been going v well last week, but I hope will be better soon.

The nightingales made a ghastly noise last night. Please send this on to K.

v.much love

yr loving

BGT

(around edge of paper)

I do hope you not feeling v limp after the measles

We feel v like Robinson Crusoe having the hut built over our heads.

Mrs.W and I may have to go off into Italy in a day or two to see about the other route.

June 12th 1917 do Capt. Spencer
2 Whitehall Court
SW
Dear K

Very many thanks for your letter of June. We are in better communication with Udine from here now which is a blessing. Such a time we had getting in-no roof on our hut so we had to sleep in the store shed for two nights — lots of insects etc, then the first night in our hut a terrific thunderstorm and torrents of water through and we had to bundle our clothes under a Burberry and I had to sleep under two umbrellas and a waterproof rug. When I woke up a large grasshopper sat looking at me! We have delightful little wooden cubicles. Mrs Watkins has been up for a few days and comes again soon. Meanwhile stores are slow arriving —I've had a terrific day yesterday dealing out thousands of cigarettes to all the batteries from 9.30 to 6 when Gen. H came down and gave us a very fierce lesson in storekeeping and accounts for 2 hours and as we were both completely exhausted we did not exactly shine at the job. He is an extraordinary person for going into every detail and now I have to deal with 6 or 7 army account books. I am sure I shall make a hideous mess of it!..... The hospital unfortunately has no nurses but we are to go over every day to take stores as they have moved from here. There is a V.A.D. Hospital in Turin Wld you like that? Supposed to be in a lovely house and then you cld come up here part of the time and probably do a good deal in this field hospital. *(Perhaps after the death of Geoffrey, Bridget was keen to have her younger sister in Italy where she could keep an eye on her.)* They are talking of moving the ... Transport and only using Italian lorries but this is not settled yet — I do not wish Humph to come here. *(There were plans to get Humphrey a job on the Italian Front in charge of railway traffic. It might have been a safer posting than on the Western front, but things were starting to go badly wrong for the Italians. Despite this B was enjoying herself))* We are the only canteen of any sort here which is <u>most</u> satisfactory and the soldiers are so delighted at the idea it does make it feel worthwhile to have come. Mona Gough thinks she is going to have another attack of appendicitis which is alarming and we may have to ship her off home which will make great complications as Mrs W may have to go off any day to see about the Salonica route...

Very much love

Your loving Bgdt

Bridget then heard from K about her planned trip to Northumberland with their bereaved uncle. Bridget was keen for them to visit their cousin, Conty Talbot, now Sitwell, who was living in her husband's family home at Barmoor, close to the Scottish border, and overlooking Holy Island. Her husband, General Sitwell, had just returned from the fiasco at Gallipoli, where, perhaps unfairly, he had been relieved of his command. He now had no future as a serving officer, which must have been a bitter blow. His wife, much younger, felt very isolated so far from her younger friends in London, so the welcome for her young cousin would have been warm. Close to Barmoor, at Ford Castle in Northumbria, lived another relative, the talented painter Lady Waterford, many of whose paintings Bridget would inherit. Meanwhile Bridget herself seems to have been thriving as she was finally in charge of something substantial.

For Haly

do Capt. Spencer

2 Whitehall Court

SW

June18 1917

Dear K

V many thanks for your letter. I am glad you are going to get a bit of a holiday and Holy Island sounds too delicious. You must go and see Barmoor and Ford. I hope you will also manage a few days on the Lincs coast with Louise and get some riding. Mrs W and I may have to go off to Lyons any day now to make arrangements for the buffets and huts on the new route. I simply loathe the idea of going in those infernal hot trains again and leaving this hut.

The work here is absolutely delightful and at last I have found the most perfect war job and what is v satisfactory is that it would be done by a sergeant and two soldiers if we weren't here. Of course I know I shall get kicked on soon by the General who gets fiercer every time and goes into every detail himself and all the other officers agree that his system of accounts, seven different books, is most fearfully complicated. It was nearly midnight last night before I had finished entering them all up. One never has 5 mins for exercise all day which may be rather a drawback — Mona (*Gough*) is very nice but not much good and makes muddles so I have to do the whole thing myself and Mrs.W is only resting and most awfully nice about letting me run the whole thing absolutely. It was lovely having a concert for 200 men out of the trenches for 3 hours. They did enjoy themselves and one said to me "It does make it feel a bit like blighty having this place to come to"!! It is great fun I have been given <u>complete</u> command of a party of soldiers who report to me at 9.30 and I am turning them on to dig a garden and grow vegetables for the batteries who have had no green food at all. A <u>very</u> nice Italian Teuen(?) Caudevalli(?) who we know well is going to the It. Embassy in London. You must make Aunt D ask him to dinner. He has lived in England and talks English. I will tell him to ring Aunt D and Aunt M up when he gets there. He will have a big blue uniform coat! The Eng officers here tell him he will wear a little red hat and a chain which makes him v wild. We are expecting a big Austrian push here soon.

V much love — I suppose you couldn't find out what the address of the dried vegetable factory at Bedford is and if they would send out supplies of vegetables?

Yr lov.BGT

Bridget clearly felt that she was doing a worthwhile job and that her talents (which were considerable as she obviously knew) were being properly used. Unfortunately her relationship with Gen H(*amilton*) was beginning to deteriorate. She had little respect for him and probably let it show. One suspects that B liked to be in charge, giving orders not receiving them.

English Canteen
Zona di Guerra
Italy
(above crossed out)
Spencer address best
June 24 1917

Dear K

Things here have been slightly difficult. Gen. H took a violent dislike to Mrs W*(atkins)* who is anything but well yet and in a state of nerves and kept on asking for unnecessary things and fair drove him wild. However luckily 3 days ago a nice Miss Broadwood arrived and Mrs W went off to the hills near here and he has calmed down again. Yesterday he discovered needless to say that I had put a whole week's list on one page meant for one day as I only finished it at 2A.M. it wasn't very surprising. One day I did 11 1/2 hours with only two breaks of 1/4 hour accounts and stores!

I am fairly dreading tomorrow as he is coming to audit the week's accounts and as I, Tad and the orderly have added the blessed books up at least 17 times and each time they have been different there is bound to be the hell of a row! G Patt is really quite nice and usually chaffs one fearfully over it all. He told Gleichen that he was quite pleased with the way the canteen was being run, which was rather a relief to hear as he has done nothing but straf me since I arrived. Funnily enough when I came into the canteen this morning I was told a new padre had arrived and found Tad. He was quite amused to find me what he chose to call 'calmly dealing out cigarettes under fire'! which was rather a highly coloured description as no shells have been over for at least ten days and there is not likely to be any fighting for ages.

Meanwhile Mrs.W and I go off to Modane leaving here Tues.night and getting there Wed. to meet Gen. Stick and make arrangements about the new route buffets which will be most thrilling, only a vile journey in this heat and with Mrs.W in her present state of nerves. Meanwhile Mona has had a collapse with the heat and the Doctor has ordered has to go back at once to England so you can imagine one is pretty pushed with it all.

I am beginning to feel like a caged animal not having been outside the gates for 10 days — one does long for exercise to keep fit. Tell me any news as one has seen no papers so far. The Tommies are so nice and delighted with the hut when they come in from the trenches. We are to go over to the Hospital 3 times a week beginning next Monday. How heavenly your trip to Holy Island will be. How I wish I was going too, to dip in the sea instead of this fearful heat and dust.

I do wish Humph could get moved onto the new route. I will see if anything can be done when I get to Modane. There are no possibilities here as I have asked. Please send this on to H. Very much love

Yr lov BGT

Do go over and see Barmoor and Ford.

What will your address be?

V Freifeld do Capt. Spencer etc

July 10 (*1917)*

Dear K

This is the first day I have had a few moments peace as having sorted stores and listed all the enormous quantity of things they are typewriting them out for me and sending round to the Batt(*allion*)s and then there will be a hideous rush again tomorrow onwards when the orders come in. We have just had 10 shells whizzing over We have got a concert to-morrow and some wounded are coming over from the hospital and others from the trenches.

It is rather peaceful having got through this big rush of stores while Hamilton is away as he comes down and rattles out innumerable orders and says "HELL" if things don't go as he likes. I hope he may have gone down to see Uncle R(*eggie)* in London. Keep this letter private.

V much love

Yr by. BGT

(At side-written over main letter)
Hope you have a delicious time at Holy Island. One misses the butterflies and no flowers here — everything dried up leaves I would be most grateful if you could send me some acid drops if such a thing is obtainable in Holy Island. Some cricket and tennis things arrived a few days ago and they have started playing cricket. I have just had a game of tennis — the first exercise for days. There is a shell hole in the middle of the court.

Lord and Lady Brownlow and guests at
Ashridge House, Hertfordshire

Alfred and Emily Talbot

Ashridge House near Little Gaddesden

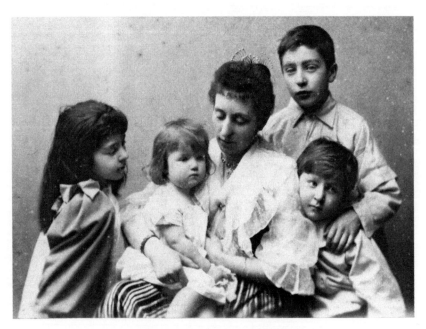

Emily with her four children

Little Gaddesden House

Humphrey, Geoffrey and Bridget

Bridget and Humphrey

WISHING YOU A HAPPY NEW YEAR from L. GADDESDEN

The Nursery at Little Gaddesden House

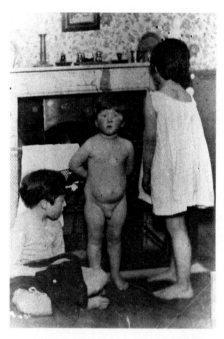

A naked Geoffrey with his siblings

Kathleen Talbot

Kathleen on the steps at Little
Gaddesden House

A family outing

Geoffrey in India

Geoffrey Talbot of the Royal Naval Air Service

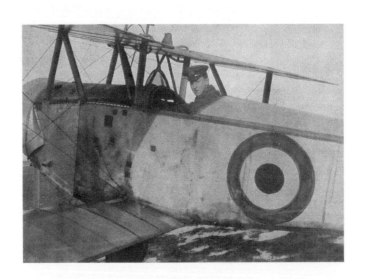

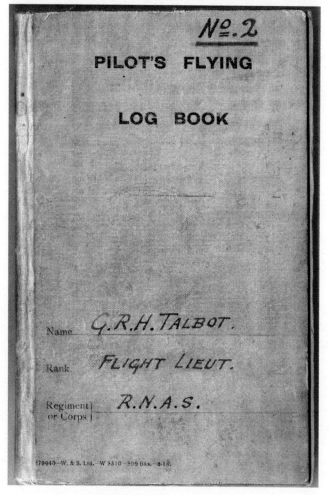

Geoffrey's pilot's log book

Letters from Geoffrey

The Church of St. Peter and St. Paul, Little Gaddesden

Geoffrey's gravestone

The War Memorial in Little Gaddesden

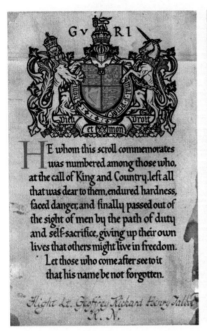

HE whom this scroll commemorates was numbered among those who, at the call of King and Country, left all that was dear to them, endured hardness, faced danger, and finally passed out of the sight of men by the path of duty and self-sacrifice, giving up their own lives that others might live in freedom. Let those who come after see to it that his name be not forgotten.

Flight Lt. Geoffrey Richard Henry Talbot R. N.

Bridget with Italian soldiers

Bridget in Italy

Young Nurse Talbot

Clopton Hospital staff

Humphrey with his parents before the war

Humphrey with Uncle Reggie in Melbourne,
Australia before the war

Humphrey at the start of the war

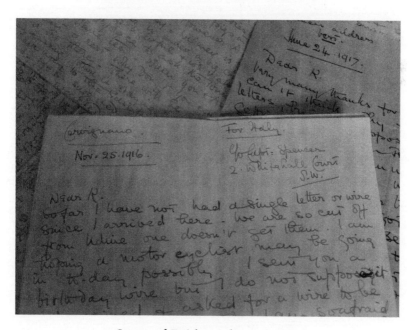

Some of Bridget's letters to K

Former patients' letters thanking Nurse Talbot

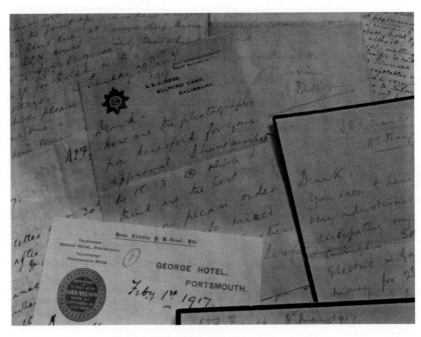

Some of Humphreys letters to K

Kathleen

Bridget in her 80's

Chapter 10

Humphrey – Bills, Bills, Bills

There was no chance of Humphrey getting leave to go to Holy Island just as he had been unable to get leave to attend his aunt's funeral at Belton. He was stuck in the mud of Flanders ferrying men, guns, ammunition, food and clothing up to the Front Line. He was also trying to keep control of affairs in Little Gaddesden, and keep up with what his sister Bridget was doing. Not content with working all hours at the Italian Front she had been plotting changes at home.

BEF France
May 21st 1917
Dear K.
Two letters from you arrived today — also enclosure about B's Co-op farm. She appears to have been corresponding with all sorts of authorities on agriculture and probably will end up replacing Ld Devenport as Food Controller if there is anything left to control. Are things really as bad as the papers make out or is it another of their political games?

Humphrey then issued innumerable instructions to his sister about paying bills. She was understandably getting confused about some of the details but received little sympathy:-

Five cheque books are child's play! If you don't look out I'll send you 2 or 3 more. Did I tell you we had left our old village and moved up much closer to the line? In fact close to my Battery. It is in the danger zone and not half such a nice place. Fritz strafes day and night which is trying and our own guns are always going off. Young, the man I am with, is quite nice and we have got a good billet in a cottage. The unfortunate landlady and her child sleep in the cellar but don't seem to mind. Weather hot and sunny but the dust is almost as bad as the mud used to be —My address remains the same.

Yr Loving H Talbot

Humphrey also corresponded regularly with his favourite aunt, Lady Talbot, Reggie's wife:-

BEF
Whitsunday 27/5/17
Dear Aunt Doobit,

I have only just heard from Uncle Reggie and from Bridget that you are miserably laid up with German measles. What a bore for you but I dare say a good rest in bed won't do you any harm. Why not make use of Gaddesden to convalesce in?

It is boilingly hot here under canvas during the day but quite cool during the night which seems very short. We haven't got at all a bad little camp though it is rather crowded......The Huns in this district are in a disagreeable mood and have been shelling the local town at intervals and their aeroplanes are also fairly active early in the morning.

I am getting the Talbot motor works to cut me a stencil of the Lion *(cut into the chalk at Whipsnade opposite Little Gaddesden)* so that I can paint it on my lorries as a private sign. It ought to look very smart and original. Our great difficulty here is the water supply and today the tanks have run dry. We have sent out a lorry to try and find another supply!

Much love and get well soon.

Yr loving
Humphrey
The Italians seem to be doing very well.

BEF France
Sunday June 10th 1917
Dear K,

Thank you for your letters of June 3rd and 6th. Also for photograph of yourself and the hospital staff. My brain is far too addled (after being out till 4 am two nights running and having to do the same tonight and indefinitely) to follow yr intricate system of transferring counters from Coutts to G Bunn and from the latter to someone else. Let's leave it as it is though I still feel I haven't paid anything.

B has written to me from Boulogne, Amiens (in the train) and Paris. She seems to be going to the front via Rome. It was very disappointing not being able to see her at Boulogne but it was impossible.

Leave is a very uncertain quantity but if I shd hear anything I wd let you know at once. It is no use making any special plans as they are bound to be upset. I haven't done anything about Italy at present. It wd be nice if we cd all get there.....

I don't know quite what to advise you about the rings, but if you know the sapphire one best I think I shd ask Uncle Addy if you may have that one.

I have such a bad memory I can't quite remember what it was like. Yr loving H. Talbot

BEF France
Thursday night 21st June, 1917
Dear K,
After 3 days without mails (owing to some muddling) your letter arrived today. It has probably been lying close by for some days as the other letters have come through much quicker. The muddling here is far worse than where we were before and it is a wonder how things get carried out.

We had to take refuge from shells in an underground dressing station the other night and I cd imagine (and see) all the kinds of cases you are constantly dealing with. I don't feel at all disposed to transfer into the R.G.A. *(The Artillery)* We get quite enough excitement as it is. At present my people have mainly to live underground as they dare not show themselves, and they also pay visits to most unpleasant places. I was a good deal struck last night by the way the strain is telling on them. Besides these disadvantages you have to be quite good at mathematics etc. We are by no means immune from Fritz's attentions even here and altogether this is a most unhealthy neighbourhood. The old place was child's play compared with this.

Much love. Yr loving H.Talbot.

Does the hospital want more funds yet?

(Humphrey was contributing regularly to Clopton Hospital funds)

I don't remember where the Motor Licence is, but probably in my Green dispatch box at LGN unless I handed the licences over to you.

The number of the motor is AR 3605. Mrs Kimm has the key of the dispatch box in her custody.

Humphrey's life was not in constant danger. He described his forays to the front as being like 'tip and run' at cricket. He was not under the threat of constant attack. Nonetheless he was certainly not in a safe 'cushy' job, and wanted family and friends back home to know it:-

BEF France

June 25th 1917

Dear K,

I am glad to say things are a bit quieter for a few days. The old place was getting too hot and we just moved in time. A shell came into the battery kitchen and also into the dressing station doing much damage. Rumour says many killed. I never knew shells come so thick and fast as they did the other night. For about a quarter of an hour there was scarcely a pause and all most unpleasantly close. One gun on the road had a pretty narrow shave as a dud shell fell right under it, but luckily did not go off.........B has discovered a possible new job for me on what she calls the Cherbourg Taranto route to the east.

I imagine it must be something to do with Railway Transport as she mentions an R.T.O. (*Railway Traffic Officer*) at Modane. She is finding out more and I hope something may come of it. It wd be nice to get a change.

Weather still unsettled and cooler which is nice.

Much love, Yr Loving H.Talbot

I see Evelyn B is to be married on July 3rd at St Georges Hanover Square.

Chapter 11

Bridget And Kathleen

By July, 1917 the military situation for the Allies had worsened, and the situation on Bridget's front was getting increasingly dangerous. None of this was yet apparent to Bridget, who had been made (or so she claimed in her 'Who's Who' entry) an 'Hon officer, Roman Grenadier Guards (apptd. following battle of Monte Santo,1917)'.

In Russia the Czar had been deposed but the offensive ordered by his Prime Minister (the Kerensky Offensive) had failed. Russia was no longer a significant military threat to Germany and shortly afterwards would be subject to a communist revolution and withdraw from the war, making peace with Germany. The threat from the east was over, and Germany and Austria no longer had to fight a war on two fronts. German soldiers could now be sent to reinforce the Austrians on the Italian front, where they had only just avoided a damaging defeat at the Eleventh Battle of the Isonzo. The battle hardened German troops introduced infiltration tactics to the Austrian front and helped work on a new offensive. Meanwhile, mutinies and plummeting morale crippled the Italian army from within. The soldiers lived in poor conditions and had engaged in attack after attack which often yielded minimal or no military gain, but for the moment there was a relative, but ominous calm. Back home, Kathleen and Earl Brownlow had finally gone on holiday in Northumberland, and seemed to have had an enjoyable time, but K had to return to Clopton Hospital and Uncle Addy went back to Belton – and mourning. Meanwhile on the Western Front there was still stalemate.

Chapter 12

Humphrey – Dark Clouds

BEF France
June 27th, 1917
Dear Aunt Doobit,
I'm afraid I have been very bad about writing, but there has been a good deal to do both in the office and on the road. We haven't moved again yet but the Battery is having a semi rest which is a blessing. The place we were in was too hot altogether. Yesterday was a lovely day and I made an expedition to a neighbouring town whether there are some rather nice old buildings but nothing much else of interest. The crops everywhere look very flourishing and they seem to grow all sorts of things including tobacco in this part of the world

Bridget has written twice since she arrived in Italy but doesn't divulge her whereabouts. She has discovered a possible new job for me on what is called the Cherbourg-Taranto route to the East. The R.T.O. (*Railway Transport Officer*) at Modane appears to have told her that he badly wanted another ASC officer to help him.

B talks of having to go (possibly) with Mrs W to see a General at Lyons who is the OC of this route, and I have asked to find out all she can. It wd be a nice change to get away from this front. The Hun is still very lively both with shells and aeroplanes, but one hears hopeful news sometimes as to his real condition. The noise of the guns isn't much annoyance. Very often you don't hear them at all. It is the whistling of the shells and the smell of gas which really makes one jumpy and uncomfortable. Weather continues unsettled and fairly cool which is a blessing when one's only shelter is a tent. Where are you now?
Yr loving
Humphrey

While keeping a brave face to his aunt, Humphrey was more open with his younger sister.

BEF France
Tuesday July 1st 1917
Dear K.,

Things are rather dismal here owing to the continued wet and cold weather, and the Hun apparently doing what he likes and going unpunished. However I suppose retribution will come sooner or later.

The papers I have are Morning Post (sometimes rather irregular) Country Life and Weekly Mirror. If you ever have a Spectator spare I wd like to see it and some cheerful paper like 'John Bull' who says the war is coming to an end about every other week.

The blackberry jam will be very good if Mrs Kimm has got any to send. Our mess President is a hopeless fool and the messing here very poor considering what we pay for extras. The Battery manages things much better and I sometimes cadge a meal off them.

For heaven's sake don't send me any cheese. It is always obtainable here in any quantity so it wd only be sending coals to Newcastle.

No more news from B but the mails are still rather deficient.

Goodnight and much love,

Yr Loving

H.Talbot

Kathleen sent her brother some photographs from Clopton Hospital. In the view of his subsequent reply she may have regretted it:-

BEF France
July 3 1917
Dear K.,

The photograph came as a shock as I didn't spot Avis (*Hodgson*) 'made up' until I read yr letter and I thought the person depicted must be some kind of a sister more or less mentally deficient.

The person on your left also looks supremely dismal. ....The food here is fairly good but rather monotonous. The Batmen here are very poor hands at cooking or they might do much better. Green vegetables are almost unknown. I wish we had got a kind neighbour like B's Italian old gentleman who grows vegetables on the Isonzo. We have had a few- very few- strawberries, currants and cherries. Mostly because they are fabulously expensive as there is such a demand. No fish since we left the other Corps but we might get some again if we are lucky. Bridget's troops ought to get dried vegetables as part of their rations. The men do here.

Apparently there seems to be infantry as well as gunners (English) on the Italian front. It is very satisfactory B having found such a congenial job. Maggot has written me a description of the garden at Gaddn and says the roses and Sweet Williams have been lovely. The roses here, much as they have been, good but there aren't many flowers except wild ones, and these in places where one doesn't want to stop long to admire them. The weather fine again and rather too hot if anything. If I have a new address I will let you know. A description of tomorrow's events will follow later! Bridget ought to be here.

Yr loving H.Talbot

Humphrey's depression soon set in again:-

BEF France
Sunday July 5th 1917
Dear K,
I am dead tired having been out every night on very trying trips and am getting to that stage when every noise makes one jump. It is very tiring never getting any real rest as when you are not up the line there is always someone worrying. Bridget has written from Modane — last letter July 3rd to say all her plans are going splendidly and she sounds very happy. I wish I cd get a job down that way.

Thanks for yr letter of July 6th posted at Grantham. The jam from Mrs Kimm, also cake from Nanny, arrived quite safely and the

F and M pate some time ago. It was excellent and a nice change. Thank you again.

Can you deal with the enclosed Bills?

I am sorry to see poor old Mrs Dennison died *(on July 10th aged 91. She was a long time resident in Little Gaddesden. Her house, Dennison Lodge, remains)*. I hope Pinnock sent a wreath. Who will take over her house I wonder?

Much love to yourself and Aunt D

Yr loving H. Talbot

BEF France

July 7th 1017

Dear K.,

This is mainly about various bills that require paying from the Joint a/c *(They were endless)*.......... Now as your brain will be fairly well addled with all these questions I will stop.

Yr Loving

H.Talbot

PS

I am most grateful for the two books you sent out as I have just finished my supply and was wondering what I should do about getting books. Please thank Aunt D. for her letter of July lst. What do you think of her suggestion about lending LGN to Nigel for his children's summer holidays? Of course they wd have to provide their own transport *(the motor being laid up owing to petrol scarcity)* and I think that they might pay for lighting — but perhaps we might do the coal as the fire wd be going in any case — Pinnock cd produce vegetables. I will write Nigel a line suggesting this and asking him to make final arrangements with you.

HT

July 10th 1917 BEF France

Dear K

(After referring to a letter from Bridget he goes on)..... I have got the caged animal feeling too as we never leave the camp except on duty and have to wait about for orders. This new Corps is about

the limit for senseless returns and never leaving one in peace. We seem to go from bad to worse everytime we move, but I suppose it will finish some day. The jam from Mrs Kimm arrived today quite safely also a cake from Nannie which it was kind of her to send. Our mess was broken up when we moved so I am again depending on the tender mercies of my batman. The books are a gt joy. The King and the P. of Wales went through this district a little time ago. Both looked very well and the King was much amused by the men stopping his car and cheering him. They blocked the road so that the motor had to pull up, and they got a good look at him. The party passed twice so we all saw them well. Much love to Aunt Doobit. Yr Loving H.Talbot

July 16th 1917 Monday BEF France
Dear K,
No more news of any leave at present and at the present moment it is unlikely I think. Some of the country we go over is absolutely blasted away — nothing left except a tree stump here and there. It is almost unbelievable until you see it. ...
Much love to you and Aunt D.
Yr loving H Talbot
I have been away 6 months now (12th July) from date of leaving London.

K. continued to act as her brother's financial secretary and ensured that he was nor deprived of treats:-

Tuesday night 24th July 1917 BEF France
Dear K,
Yes the pheasant pate from F and M arrived and was excellent. Many thanks again. I think I have acknowledged its arrival and disposal in two previous letters but never mind. Toby writes from 28CG to say several people have been to look at the house and one lady said she wd come again, so I hope there may be a let later on. He says a bomb hit the Bank of England and also the GPO and much damage was done in the East End but none in the Chelsea district. If you get a chance some more books wd be very

welcome as the life here is practically imprisonment as one cannot leave the camp without asking and there is nowhere to go if one does. You must charge me up with anything you send out. The books and papers all go on to the men who very much appreciate them. They too practically get no amusement except a game of cards or a game they play with halfpennies on the principle of knucklebones. Last Sunday there was a Church parade, a concert and a cricket match which was a nice change for those able to get away. I have had a few nights in, which has been a rest, but this hot and thundery weather takes it out of me, and being alone is rather dull. The other people here are not very attractive, and I often wish Crawford was back as companion. This group is ruled by two Captains as it comprises several columns, I have discovered a Bulford friend in one of the other groups and hope to see him occasionally, but unfortunately it is 2 miles away.

I sometimes manage some sleep in the daytime, but usually it is too hot to do much good, to say nothing of the noise of passing vehicles, camp noises etc. Yesterday the Medical Officer came round to inspect and we have been carrying out his recommendations.

Your last lot of good things from Fortnum and Mason have kept me going and Aunt D's soups have been most useful.

It is good news that another parcel is on its way. The cocoa mixture is very good and I have used some Aunt D sent me out. We get plenty of sugar, condensed milk of various brands and margarine but the latter is very oily in this hot weather so I do without it or make jam a lubricant for the head.

This is nearly always good and not the war mixture there is such a fuss about in England, but we have to be 'sparing' as Nannie wd say. The apple rings are an excellent idea and whitebait and asparagus sound delicious!

Any fruit or vegetables are welcome as other than dried figs we never get any. Bridget is still working away at finding out if there is any possibility of me getting down that way, but there doesn't appear to be much prospect of moving. However one never knows what may turn up.

Rumble, rumble in the distance. Fritz seems busy too. We just moved from our last camp in time as the very next day he strafed it, and has done so again since. The Spectator you said you had ordered to come out hasn't turned up as yet. It wd be very interesting to see what they say about the political changes in Germany. How disappointing the Russians are, and the Italians seem to have gone to sleep again. It's about time they took Trieste. Now I must go to bed. Your holiday seems very quickly over if you go back to Clopton 23rd (yesterday).

Much love. Yr Loving Humphrey Talbot

In his next letter Humphrey actually thanked K for her help with bills. She must have been taken aback:-

Sunday July 29th, 1917 BEF France

Dear K.,

Thanks for your letter of the 21st with enclosures, and also for having dealt with so many bills. They always come in a swarm about Midsummer.

We all trooped up to Siege Park this morning as the Major wanted to have a photograph taken of all the officers. It won't be a success I'm afraid as a heavy thunderstorm came on in torrents of rain which isn't good for photography. It is beastly muggy and damp this af/n in consequence. We had an air raid on Friday night. Most unpleasant as the bomb dropped close by and one felt so helpless. Last night there was another alarm but luckily it didn't develop into anything here. Later in the night we were all woken up for a gas attack which was thicker in some places than others. So life is not altogether peaceful. People in England ought to be grateful that at any rate they are spared gas attacks. There was a rumour yesterday that our airmen had dropped bombs on Berlin. I hope they may have done so as if the Germans get a taste of their own inventions it will shorten the war as much as anything.

All sorts of other rumours about too, but probably they are all more or less untrue. We must 'wait and see'.

I wonder if Pinnock has managed to get in the hay? Harvest is going on here. Much love

Yr loving H Talbot

8pm

Mails just arrived and your 2 letters one from York station 23rd (posted at Grantham) and the other from Clopton 25th

Very many thanks for a parcel from F and Mason which also arrived tonight. I am going to have a whitebait supper!

That ready mixed cocoa is an excellent idea and very useful out here. I shall become quite fat with all the things you have sent me.

Pinnock reports hay being got up and good weather so far which he hopes will continue. I am sorry to say he says Kitty has got lame in her off hind leg. They have had the vet who gave G Bunn some stuff to rub in but at present she is still lame. Otherwise she feeds well and is out in the paddock, but is not fit to work. I am afraid it is possibly old age and it will be difficult to get a substitute.

HT

Sunday August 5th 1917 BEF France *(part of this letter is eaten away)*

Dear K.,

Books galore from you keep arriving and this is to convey my thanks for such a delightful library. I have been reading 'The Green Flag' and other stories which are excellent though creepy.

The guns are at it again and making a terrific row. I can't think how any human being survives when they all let loose. Since last Sunday it has poured almost incessantly and you can imagine the state of mud and slime, especially horse lines. Today it has at last turned fine and dried up extraordinarily quickly.

Did I thank you for 2 other books and several newspapers? If not herewith many and grateful thanks.

Sir D Haig sent round a very cheerful message a few days ago.

Yr loving H Talbot

28 CG is to be painted outside in the near future.

There is then a gap of five weeks before the next letter from Humphrey which has survived:-

Wedny Sept 12th, 1917 BEF France
Dear K.,
At last the mails are beginning to get straight again and a batch of letters arrived this mng including yrs of the 2nd. Very many thanks for the F and M things which arrived a day or two ago. They are excellent especially the plum pudding. If you could get me a set of draughts they wd be much appreciated by the men. The set I gave them is in constant use. Cards I think they have got but probably another pack wd come in useful. You must keep an a/c of these things and also of the books so that I can settle up with you. Some more books soon wd come in useful. Tell yr bookseller he puts the wrong paper cover on outside and the other day thinking I was going to read 'Dr Nikole' I found it was quite another book. The weather has been fine on the whole here lately and very hot. Today winds, and more like rain.
What do you think of the latest Russian news? They are a hopeless lot.
(The Czar had been deposed and there were revolts in the army and navy. The Bolsheviks had not yet taken over but it was becoming clear that Russia would quickly cease to be an effective ally.)
Has Aunt Doobit got back from Strathpeffer? If so give her my love and tell her I hope she is much better after the baths. Nothing else to write about.
Yr loving. H.Talbot

Humphrey's hopes were now pinned on his elder sister finding him a more congenial job in Italy, but she soon had other priorities.

Chapter 13

Bridget – The Money Runs Out

In Italy things were not going well for Bridget. On September 17th she wrote a brief note to K saying she was going to Bologna, and soon after sent this next, undated, letter in which she is frank about her disappointment at the turn of events. She sounds exhausted. What had happened to upset Bridget?

It seems to have been that Mrs. Henry Watkins had run out of money, with what Bridget feared would be unfortunate consequences for her. In a report she wrote to the War Office from Rome in April 1918 Mrs Watkins said this:-

After two years of heavy expenditure, I found that my funds were insufficient to carry on my various undertakings and therefore, on September 22nd 1917, I was glad to join the Red Cross and Order of St John which had already and most kindly and substantially supported our work during the stress of the last months.

It seems that Bridget feared that the independence of action and relative autonomy she had achieved under a private, ad hoc, organization, would be clawed back by the bureaucracy of a longer established and more formally structured organization:-

The British Red Cross Society
And the Order of St John of Jerusalem
In England
12 Via Carducci
Udine
Sept 17th
I'm on way back from Bologna
Dear K
At last I can write by the ordinary post though I suppose I cannot tell you exactly what is doing. Anyhow my job has suddenly come

to an end and it may be more possible for Ronald Storrs to take on the job than for me. I have not been given the sack but it is no use staying on if there is nothing to do. It will take a few days to wind things up and then I shall come to England. It is absolutely sickening just as we had settled down and got everything running smoothly and a huge lot of stores had come in — such a bore having to look out for a new job. The last few days have been indescribable and eventually I had to dash off on a perfectly useless journey to Faenza with Mrs W to finally settle with Gray about the other huts and he failed to turn up. Mrs W has stayed on but I had to get back as I only had 24 hours leave — H(*amilton*) only told me I cld go at 2.30 having told me I was to stand to for orders till 1 o'c. I only had time to throw a few things into a box and rush to the station 20 miles in H's motor. I am now bringing back despatches to H- I am told they are very important. I am sure I shall lose them. I nearly missed the 6.15a.m train of course- only had a few hours sleep in the last 3 or 4 days as there has been such a terrific amount to do and now again the next few days will be worse- I am just about tired out. Please stop everything you ordered coming and let Lady Salisbury know at once. If things come I can get them down to the drifters or other people passing East. It is v unexpected but such is war. I am afraid the plan for H(*umphrey*) is also unlikely to come off as I do not now think Mrs W will see Gray. We came to the conclusion the huts and canteen were not a neccisity(*sic*) though the CO. on the spot strongly urged it. Taranto may still come off — but it is too long to explain all this. In the ordinary course of events I might have had 24 hours leave in Venice but all that is off now. Please send this on to Aunt D and I will wire when I am likely to turn up in England. It is all very disgusting and maddening. V Much love
Yr lov
BGT

Chapter 14

Humphrey – Promotion

Back in France Humphrey was still hoping for that transfer to Italy, but his diet had certainly improved:-

Tuesday 25th Sept 1917 BEF France
Dear K,
I must thank you for a whole heap of things which have arrived the last day or two. All the good things from F and Mason, also the new books and the games, which will get plenty of use as soon as their arrival is discovered. My office staff sat up most of last night trying to solve the Domino puzzle, but so far they have only got 10 on every side except one and cannot manage the remaining side. The book with a picture outside of a Judge apparently looking for fleas down a lady's back sh'd be most thrilling. I have just finished reading Paul Patoff (Marian Crawford) which is quite a good story.
Maggot wrote to me yesterday and sent some excellent gingerbread nuts and blackberry jelly wh is very kind of her. I must write and express my gratitude. We are having splendid weather and very hot in the middle of the day. When will the Huns agree with General Smuts that they are beaten and it is time to finish this foolish game?
Much love. Yr loving
H.Talbot

But the war continued, the job in Italy did not transpire, and Humphrey's gloom returned
He wrote to K on October 1st 1917:-

BEF France
Another month gone and I wonder if we are any nearer the end. Our new camp is quite nice and pretty country for a change. There

is a hill close by and a really beautiful view in all directions including the front. But our own work isn't pleasant and they are asking too much of the lorries and men. I had an exciting time ystdy as fritz saw our lorries and began shelling and it was some time before we cd bolt as he was putting the shells so close. The lorry had several hits through it and every moment I expected to see it blown to bits. We shivered in a dug out nearby. Also there is no peace these moonlight nights as Fritz drops bombs everywhere and all night long. I hadn't put up my tent five minutes before a nose cap from one of our Anti Aircraft shells came whizzing down just outside. The men dug it up as a souvenir. There are always bits flying about when any firing is going on. I don't know how leave stands in this Corps *(the 10th)* but possibly having moved again will spoil any chances that they were. The 'rather more responsibility' is hanging fire and I hope won't come off.
(Had H been promised a promotion?)
Thank you, in anticipation, for all the things F and Mason are sending. The food has been bad lately so they will be useful.
Several Insurance reminders have come to me so I have paid them as they are urgent. Now I must have a little snooze as I was up most of the night on top of a trip up the line during the day.
Yr loving
H Talbot
Thanks for yr 2 letters of Sept 23rd and 25th

Oct 8th 1917 BEF France
Dear K,
Rain, Rain, Rain, which isn't cheerful but with all the good things from Mrs Kimm and F and Mason I have been able to have a birthday feast. Our lovely weather has departed and it has turned very cold and wet. Your letter arrived today so it couldn't have been better timed, and the parcels last night. Are you or B responsible for sending them? Whichever it is very many thanks for such a heap of good things. Maggot's blackberry jelly and ginger nuts were quite excellent tell her if she is meeting you at Gaddn.

Thank you too for the book which is coming from Bumpers(?) If not out these long evenings one is very glad of something to read. Also thanks for another Spectator......

(Then H lets slip that he has been promoted — to acting Captain, but he shows little enthusiasm, or perhaps he is just being modest).

......Leave appears fairly remote still, though I have heard of one man with about 18 months out here getting some. I expect the War will finish first. It is quite true I got promotion but as it is by seniority and there are thousands ahead of me on the list, it is merely a question of waiting. Your string band sounds very nice and I hope it will be a success. Does the Clopton hospital have want any more funds as I think another subs must be about due.

Much love
Yr loving H.Talbot

In his next letter Humphrey expresses concern about what is happening at home, or rather in London, and frustration that there is no end in sight to the conflict:-

Monday October 15th 1917 BEF France
Dear K,
Very many thanks for the book 'Sonia' which has arrived, and also for plum pudding and pate de perdreaux and your letter of Oct 9th. One of my men has just returned from London off leave (after 18 months out here) reports that the damage done by the air raids was a good (Chelsea end of Grosvenor Road etc) deal worse than the papers made out, and he says people are getting very uneasy. I have written to Aunt D and tried to persuade her when the next moon comes in a few days and air raids are likely again, to go to Gaddesden with her household for the dangerous period as it is no use sitting still and waiting to be bombed.
There is almost as much danger from our own anti-aircraft shells as from the Hun.

I wonder how much longer we have got to hold on? The politicians keep on lengthening it by their silly speeches. I thought we were fighting to regain Belgium but now it seems to be Alsace Lorraine as well and probably something else after that.

No other news

Yr loving H.Talbot

Chapter 15

Kathleen – Mentioned
In Dispatches

There was good news for Kathleen in October 1917. Her outstanding work at Clopton had been recognized. On the 25th, Aunt Doobit, Uncle Reggie's wife, wrote from 22, Grosvenor Road, Westminster:-

Dearest Kathleen,
No, I had not seen, but I have now — congratulations to you darling and Avis (*Hodgson*) too on being 'mentioned in dispatches'. I retrieved Tuesday's Times which contained you, but Monday's in which Avis's name must have come — could not be found.
I suppose you have sent the list out to H and B — as they ought to see it. I am very proud of my nieces and have told Uncle Reggie who, I am sure, will be hugely delighted. This comes of sticking to your good work in the <u>same place</u>!!

Aunt Doobit went on to describe the bombing of London which so bothered Humphrey :-

All I heard of the last (*German*) raid was one huge explosion over the river and as there was no firing and no police whistles I concluded it must be some munitions or other factory blown up — and went to sleep! And only next morning found that there had been a raid and an aerial torpedo dropped in Piccadilly had blown in every window of Swan and Edgar and other shops. The one I heard I think must have been at Camberwell when damage was done to small streets and poor people killed. Seven or eight were killed opposite Swan and Edgars. It is clearing up for them this evening!! Hope we shan't have them.

Much love. I hope you will soon get a medal.

Yr loving Aunt Doobit.

Do tell Avis how proud I am of her too!

One wonders how Humphrey and Bridget, ten and eight years older than their 'baby sister', reacted to the news of her decoration? At this stage Bridget had not had her work recognised officially in the UK, and Humphrey received only the usual campaign medals. Humphrey however was generous in writing. On October 31st he congratulated K for being 'mentioned in dispatches', and on November 19th he even complimented her on her bookkeeping. At this stage K still seems to be thinking of joining her sister in Italy, to where Humphrey was of course also trying to get posted. He wrote on Nov 26th, 1917 that 'I have got quite a good move on about your thing'.

After this we hear no more about Kathleen's war.

Chapter 16

Bridget – Homeward Bound?

In October 1917, a frustrated Bridget was still in north east Italy as the Germans and Austrians began to build up for the offensive. She felt underemployed, but would soon be running for her life:-

Oct 5 1917

Dear K

I still don't know what is going to happen but I hope anyhow perhaps to get some leave about Nov 1st. It may be for good or it may be worthwhile returning for the few people who remain but it is doubtful. It is pouring tonight — such a thunderstorm - Thank you most awfully for some delicious Fort(*num*) and Mason peppermint and biscuits and chocolate. We have had several air raids here these last few days. You seem to have had a lot in London. I wish Aunt D(*oobit*) would go away for full moons (*when most of the air raids took place over London*). The rats are infernal and I believe there must be a dead one under the floor of my room. We had a cricket match yesterday and a concert. As no extra transport is allowed one very sporting Batt(*allion*) walked all the way back 12 miles they all enjoyed themselves hugely. Sir Sam Hoare who is on the staff in Rome turned up — Maud is in Rome and might possibly come up here. He has been out in Russia and is not hopeful about events there. A party of M.P.s are arriving round sometime soon including Aubrey Herbert and Evelyn Cecil. It is funny seeing the sort of people who belong to London drawing rooms turn up in these parts! Please ask Aunt D if it is possible to stop all the woollies etc for the time being. The blankets are of course provided by the W.O. but I only thought some extras would be most welcome judging by the cold weather of last year. However none may be necessary now.

Much love
Yr love
BGT

A strange calm seemed to prevail on the Italian front. The Austro German offensive had not started. Bridget was waiting to go home and had much less to do. Fortunately she had been able to receive packages from Kathleen. No-one seemed to realise that disaster was about to overwhelm them:-

Oct 12th 1917 (*no address*)
Dear K

Just a hurried line to thank you for your last letter and a most lovely lot of games which are enormously appreciated. There was a tremendous run on the cards as they are unobtainable out here and I was able to give the old ones to the trains. I still do not know whether I am to come back here or not for the winter. Gen.H(*amilton*) doubtful whether it would be worthwhile. Anyhow it will be shut for Nov. and I suppose I shall know before I go. We have had a lot of people in the hut the last few days so we had a whist drive yesterday — and today we had indoor sports — biting at sticky apples on strings etc. I had the first walk I had had since I got here today about 1½ miles and I am absolutely stiff and fagged out as a result. It is fearfully cold and damp now. Mrs Watkins away for a holiday at the lakes. I can't tell which day I shall get back but will wire when I start.
Now must stop
Much love
Yr by
BGT

Oct 6 1917
(*no address*)
Dear Aunt D(*oobit*)
Very many thanks for yr letter and for seeing about things for me. I think it wld be as well to hold up everything for the moment but

I wish you cld send me just a few parcel posts of scarves and socks which no doubt some society would supply. Perhaps after all it would be as well to send also a thousand other things by train, socks, helmets, mittens, jerseys etc as one can't have too many in the wet here and if necessary one can always pass on to the sailors and drifters who don't get particularly well supplied in these days. If no more trains are coming which they wd know I suppose I don't see how they will get here except by parcel post so I really don't know what to suggest and everything is so uncertain. It is really bitter here today — no stoves in our hut and lots of the windows without glass and large cracks between the boards. Snow on the mountains. I expect I shall get back the beginning of Nov. whether for good remains to be seen. I had the most terrific straffing today from Hamilton for having gone to see some of our men in the infectious Hosp. I asked all the Eng and It authorities first of all. I found a man who the It Doc thought very ill and sent a message to the E.doctor. This unfortunately got to H.Q. who now threatens either to lock me up as infectious for 3 weeks or send me straight home. I don't think either will be carried out unless the As insist on it as the cases were not really in the least infectious.

(letter continues scribbled on side)

Later Oct 8

Still no definite orders. It is a gt question with all the uncertainty of everything and no transport whether I shall return or not in Dec-I shall aim at being back the beginning of Nov -will Uncle Addy be at Belton then?

V much love

Yr by.

BGT

Oct 17 1917

Dear Aunt Doobit

The rain and damp here is awful and tonight Mrs Nott who was here for a few days has a temp. of 104 and we are v much afraid it may be pneumonia and all the hut is ringing with damp and pouring rain. I have got an ambulance coming for her tomorrow to take her to Villa Tranto but it will be a job getting her over the mud to the ambulance dry — we have no stoves so far but after asking 6 or 8 times I have at last secured some for tomorrow. Everyone has been most kind helping and Miss Wood is here who knows something about nursing although very young. On the top of this we have a huge concert on tomorrow and now at 9.30 pm we have just been asked to do a supper for a departing Camp Commandant for 40 of his men at 9pm after the concert. Ted has an early service in the hut at 7am and we have to do breakfast for the men afterwards so it will be a day of action and we shall have to take turns at being up all night.

Now must stop and wade through 1½ foot of water to our hut.

Much Love Yr Lovng

BGT

Our huts still leak and no window shuts and swarms of rats but anyhow I hope there will be no air raid or shells till we get Mrs Nott safely off tomorrow.

Bridget was not to get her leave. The Italian Front suddenly collapsed, and the Austrians and Germans poured down onto the Venetian plain. Her brother and sister did not hear what had happened to her for some days.

Chapter 17

Humphrey – Thank Heavens For Fortnum And Mason

Wednesday Oct 31st 1917 BEF France
9.30 pm
Dear K

Very many thanks for many different things. Some more books arrived a day or two ago but we have been busy lately and I am getting behindhand with reading so please don't send anymore for the time being. A long lost box of things — Bath Olivers, whitebait, shortbread, Dorset butter, chocolate rations, honey etc from F and Mason has also arrived but whether from B or you I don't know. The box was addressed to 'B' Corps so it must have started ages ago. I am afraid I have bombarded you with nothing but bills lately.

Many Congratulations on being 'Mentioned in Despatches'. It is about time they did thank you after all the time you have been at Clopton. Herewith the list which you ask me to return.

Thank you for all the things which are coming from F and Mason. They are always welcome though you send me such a lot that I have to keep sharpening my teeth to get through it!

The Zepps the other day seem to have been everywhere and Pinnock reports that bombs fell at Luton, Bletchley and Dunstable and shook the windows at home.

Have you any news of Bridget? She hasn't written since the 16th and with this Italian defeat I feel rather anxious as to what has happened to her. According to the papers the Huns and Austrians can't be very far from Udine which she sometimes goes to. Let me know if you hear anything. Of course she talked of starting homewards about Nov 1st so she may have been extra busy clearing up and not had time to write. Weather rather better lately, but up country nothing can describe the desolation and mud. Everything swimming in water. Fritz buzzing around somewhere confound him.

Much love, Yr loving

H. Talbot

Chapter 18

Bridget – Running For Her Life

So where was Bridget? Running for her life.

On the Italian Front on October 24, 1917 the calm had been shattered.

The Austrians and Germans launched the battle of Caporetto with a huge artillery barrage followed by infantry using infiltration tactics, bypassing Italian strong points and attacking the rear. At the end of the first day the Italians had been forced to retreat twelve miles to the Tagliamento river. Three hundred thousand Italians were taken prisoner and all of the gains of the previous two and a half years were reversed.

Thereafter the Italian war was fought in the lowlands of the Piave River valley, close to Venice, which seemed likely to be captured at any moment.

Since the war had begun Italy had suffered six hundred thousand casualties. Because of these losses the Italian Government now called up all males who were eighteen years old or over. More British, French and American troops were also sent to bolster the front lines and strategic materials were shipped across.

At this point Bridget was in charge of the canteen at the Villa Freifield near Gradisca, where, according to Mrs. Watkins' report, she was organizing sports, concerts, whist drives and entertainments. After the German Austrian breakthrough her friends and family heard nothing from her for some days. There was confusion and panic everywhere. Eventually Kathleen received a letter:-

Nov 4 1917

Dear K

I am afraid I have been very bad about writing — but we have all been so exhausted added to the v trying times and not knowing what was going to happen to us one simply hasn't had the energy to write. We got no orders so cld do nothing but wait. Now suddenly today we are to start off two huge canteens one for the French here and the other at Pavia for the English. I am to do the Eng one though in some ways I wd rather have done the French and not had the responsibility of the other as I feel pretty tired out to start off on a new and big job and it will be hideously difficult to get any stores in this turmoil. Mrs Watson and I went off to Pavia today to see Gen Grey and he said it was the one thing most awfully wanted at the moment. After the awful doings at the front, - three or four days of the most head-splitting shells over and near and then the retreat, one wants a bit of rest on the top of 5 months without a pause. However it wd be absurd to go back to England now even for 2 or 3 weeks just at the moment when all kinds of work will be terrific. Tomorrow I was asked to go to Turin with a soldier to get through a lot of motor stores and Red X stores but now I have to go again to Pavia which is sad as I had so hoped to go to the Eng. Hosp. at Turin and hear news of our people at the front. Ted is I believe safe and I have wired to Fantham. Some of the patients from the hosp. had to walk 40 miles — 2 typhoid cases — and only had 2 sardines and a bit of chocolate. However they are none the worse. One man who had been through Mons said it was a cake walk compared to this! The sad part was that we cd so easily have taken some on our motor if anyone had realised how quick the whole thing was to be as they only started a few hours after us. Knowing the roads I was able to get our motor along quite away from the crush till we got to the Tagliamento. Our big gun was only able to get over the bridge by the officer standing at the head of the bridge and shooting down the crowd. Several It(alian) officers have committed suicide and there is a great mystery over the fate of Capello. It is all too awful. V Trento nurses had to walk 20 and 30 miles in the pouring rain. Our Batt. men marched along singing - goodness only knows what will happen now in the next few weeks or days the fate of Italy will be decided. Some of the Batt. officers had to shoot ducks and chickens with their revolvers to provide food for the men as they went along.

I am afraid this letter is very scrappy but the V.T. people will tell you so much more. Grey told me he had applied for H*(umphrey)* but there hadn't been a vacant job on the line at the moment. He thinks he will arrive here where the canteen is to be in a few days and if not he will make special application for him. It will be extraordinary if he does turn up. What do you feel about coming out if he does? There are bound to be huge hospitals and anyhow there is one in Turin. I may have to go there one day soon and will report on it. If you wd like it cd get Hamilton to wire for you to the W*(ar)*.O*(ffice)*. if I can get a letter up to him. Yesterday Uncle Tom and Aunt Agnes turned up here but not in this hotel. I am to go and have luncheon with them one day - such an extraordinary collection from the War Zone turn up here. Ashby, Sperduza Bonocuie and Sprainger and all Villa Trento and all of us. V much love. It is tiresome getting no leave. If one had just started all wd have been well but it wd be too feeble to go away now.

Yr loving

BGT

This address for present.

Nov 5 1917

Dearest K

Just a hurried line in case you didn't get the other to say I saw Gen Grey yestday who said H*(umphrey)* was probably on his way anyhow. If not he would arrange for his transfer at once if H wld wire me here the number of his division. Yr young man.....
(Who was this? A boyfriend of K's or just someone she thought attractive?) ......the one the papers suggested is where we start the new big English canteen tomorrow and we saw him at HQ today. You really <u>must</u> come out.

I discovered this evening that I am called 'General Talbot'— I knew I had a nickname but had never found out what it was. We leave here Wed but won't be so very far off so this is the best address for the present.

V much love

Yr loving

BGT

Have had no letters for 3 weeks of any sort — only Ant D's wire on Sat or Sun. Please thank her for it v much.

Hotel du Nord
Et Des Anglais
Gare Centrale
Milan
(headed paper)
Nov 6 1917
Dear K
Everything is in such a state of uncertainty that I can't give any definite idea of what we are going to do. First of all we are told to get everything ready to start this canteen for arriving Eng at Pavia thousands at a time. Then when we have collected all our stores and everything ready Gen Alexander talks of packing us all on a truck and moving us further forward to the railhead. All this uncertainty is very trying after 5 weeks of it. I am frightfully disappointed this evening as it was on the cards that I was to go to Venice with Teresa to help her to rescue things from her house there but unfortunately someone else has to go to Padua so I can't go. It is sickening. Meanwhile some of our people saw Ld Monson yesterday and he reported that Hamilton was writing to the effect that I was to go to England, but as he doesn't know about the new canteen I don't know what will happen — I will let you know as soon as I know anything definitely.
V much love
Yr lovn
BGT
Aunt D's letter came today

Bridget had also written to her brother, who in normal situations was a great worrier and this was far from normal, but her letters to him had been delayed, as had those of his other sister:-

Chapter 19

Humphrey – A Flanders Christmas

Nov 4th 1917 BEF France

Dear K,

Many thanks for your letter of the 20th October. You seem to have heard from B much later than I have. The 'Morning Post' reports the party as safe in Milan, *(he enclosed a cutting)* and tonight I had a postcard from Aunt D saying she had a telegram from B from Milan where she was awaiting further orders. I wonder now if she will stop in Italy and return home as she intended? The air is full of rumours and possibly B might get a lift in a lorry.

It has been much warmer the last day or two, but today a white mist and regular November. The autumn colouring is good in places specially some Turkish oaks in a little (destroyed) village near here.

Pinnock has sent me some very good apples and pear weighing 1½lbs.

Goodnight. Yr loving
H.Talbot

The cutting referred to by Humphrey is from the Morning Post of the 1st Nov and is headed :-

The British Red Cross
Most of the Units accounted for Italian Front, Oct 3 1st

Part of it reads:-

......Mrs.Watkins, the head of the English canteens, and all her party have been sent to <u>Milan</u> *(H has underlined this in red).*
After having set fire to all stores, the Sub-Commissioner for the British Red Cross had had all his units centred at the places chosen by Headquarters for reorganization. There they were met by Lord Monson, who transferred the units further south, wishing that their reorganisation should be carried out without its interfering with the work of the Italians.
Of seventy ambulances only six were taken by the enemy, while eight were abandoned on the way because they were disabled. Only one man was badly wounded, being hit in the neck. Two units, also twelve nurses of the second and third units, as well as twelve English nurses of the first unit, have not yet reached the concentration post, but it is believed they have been delayed owing to the difficulty of transit. The head of the first unit and the head of the radiographic unit have stayed behind to collect the missing.

Tuesday Nov 6th 1917 BEF France
Dear K,
At last I have heard from Bridget dated Milan Oct 30th. She seems to have had an adventurous journey partly by ambulance and partly by hospital train and is now awaiting further orders. She hears that the French frontier is closed so does not think there is much chance of getting home at present. I have told her to keep me posted up in her movements as I believe it is possible to get 2 or 3 days 'Paris' leave if the authorities can be persuaded to grant it. If so we might possibly arrange a meeting. Thank you ever so much for the F and M things which arrived yesty — Biscuits, chocolate, sardines, turtle soup etc. All very good. Also for 4 more books from a new shop in Stamford. I have been trying a mixture of Ghost stories and 'Sonia'! There are all sorts of rumours about Italy, but nothing very definite and of course if there was my tongue wd be tied. The men wd like to go

I think — Anywhere almost for a change from this vile front which they loathe.
Yr loving
H.Talbot

Meanwhile Humphrey had to start preparations for Christmas, not in Little Gaddesden or in Italy, but in the mud of Flanders:-

November 9th 1917 BEF France
Dear K,
With regard to number of men in my column, I see the Govt. is making an arrangement for everyman out here to have ½ lb of Xmas pudding and is therefore asking the public not to send out puddings at Xmas. Otherwise I had intended to order some from F and Mason or elsewhere. The oranges and cigarettes wd. be much appreciated but I think I ought to do this and not you.
The numbers vary between 36 and 44 according to circumstances, as some are nearly always away on detached duty.
No further news from Bridget. The Italians seem utterly demoralized and rumours are going round of a separate peace, but this seems hardly likely. We are being badly let down by our Allies. However Passchendaele and Gaza are comforting.
(The appalling losses at Passchendaele had not at that point been revealed. However the victory at Gaza in the Middle East was real enough and would lead to the capture of Jerusalem and the defeat of Germany's ally Turkey.)
Now I must do some letter censoring so goodnight.
Yr loving
H.Talbot

November 15th 1917 BEF France
Dear K,
I think I had better write some days beforehand so that this can reach you on or about your birthday to wish you very happy returns of the day and every good wish. Let's hope we shall someday get back to normal birthdays and Christmasses as otherwise we shall quite forget how to celebrate them. Fortnum

and Mason should be sending you some Chocolate Caramels and Rahat Loukoumin*(?)* which I hope you will like and not have snatched from you by the Food Controller. If there is anything else you particularly want let me know as the above is a very measly present.

Very good news was rumoured here yesty, but so far nothing to confirm it in the newspapers, but of course there has hardly been time. All we know is that there has been a terrific bombardment going on.

I see the Huns claim to have crossed the Piave so I'm afraid it is touch and go for Venice which is only about 20 miles off. Bridget wrote to me from Milan dated 6th Nov asking me to wire my address etc. I hope my telegram will have reached you and that you have done it on my behalf. Grey seems to be getting a move on at last and if he succeeds I shall be truly thankful to get away from him*(?)*. We keep going from bad to worse. Our address is now 252 SBAC 3 Siege Park 9th Corps. Did B. tell you that your <u>very</u> special young man from Windsor is waiting for you in Milan! You will certainly have to come out if the family party scheme comes off. B. has seen him at H.Q. She talks of Hotel Tre Re at Pavia as possibly being her address, but all letters and telegrams for the present are to go to the Hotel du Nord Milan.

I had forgotten there was a possible hotel in Pavia, but perhaps we didn't go into the town when we went to see the Certora (before the War). It was about 12 or 15 miles by motor from Milan. We had luncheon at a dirty little inn but had some excellent Asti Spumante. I had a nice muddy morning at my Battery yesty falling in and out of shell holes, but happily Fritz left us alone when we were there. It isn't a spot to linger in.

Well very much love and as happy a birthday as possible and lots more happier ones to come.

Yr loving,
H.Talbot

Chapter 20

Bridget – Interpreter

B was still trying to fix a job for K in Italy as well, what she called 'your thing'. Unsurprisingly she wanted the three remaining members of the Talbot family to see out the war together in a country which they all loved, and which, despite the recent Austrian advance, was a safer location than Flanders:-

Nov 26th 1917
Dear K.,
Since writing I have got quite a good move on about your thing. Sir L.T. Head of the B.R.C. will be here in a few days and although I am going on to the railhead today two of our people will be here and I am to be sent for the moment he arrives. I sent you a p card to this affect this afternoon but sent this as well to say don't sign on to anything else too quickly as I think it more than likely they will accept Mrs On and staff. I am also to see the gen of the R.A.M.C. in a few days who is the ultimate authority for all *(?)* so I think between them we ought to get something through. Where do you want to be, Rome, Florence, Taranto, San Remo, Turin? I have been offered a home at San Remo. I saw G this morning and he promised again to get something for H in the next few weeks but at the moment he does not know what men he wants. He was extremely kind and I think really means to do it!
(Bridget said that she had sent H an Italian phrase book so that he could prepare for the new assignment. She of course was quite fluent in Italian)
We are being used all day as interpreters for the R*(ailway)*.T*(ransport)*.O*(fficer)*s. Have just been translating orders from H.Q. Most amusing.
(The second page of this letter is lost and so there is no signature.)

Chapter 21

Humphrey – Where's Bridget?

30th Nov 1917 BEF France

Dear Aunt Doobit,

The china from Harrods has duly arrived and it is just what I wanted. Very many thanks for your getting it for me. Only one little bit was chipped but it is a marvel how the things escaped as they were badly packed and the box itself smashed to smithereens and all the paper torn off.

K. says she is straining every nerve to get out to Italy and appears to have thought I might be on my way there. But I am still here for the time being and nothing more has been heard of Bridget since she last wrote from Milan on the 6th Nov.

We have got quite a nice little lorry standing on our own wh. is much nicer than being under the eye of HQ and I have made friends with the O.C. Water Column near by who has got a car, so we can occasionally have a joy ride with business combined. Lovely day today and the weather is very kind on the whole lately. Mrs. Vivian has found a sub tenant for 28 CG in the shape of a Captain Douglas Hall

so all is well — though of course in any case she wd have been responsible for the Rent.

Now goodnight

Yr loving,

H. Talbot

Saturday December 1st, 1917 BEF France

Dear K

At last I have had a postcard from B. dated 23rd Nov and posted from Legnago, *(Verona)*. Her address is c/o A.P.O.S 101 BEF Italy. She appears to have been expecting to see me, but 'now it seems uncertain whether you will come or not'. I shall wait a few days and hope I may get the wire I asked for and see Grey. She says she is moving forward she doesn't know where. - They are being made official. She hopes to get leave as soon as they are established and to see me in Paris if not in Italy (subject of course to me getting a Paris leave). She has only had one of my letters and no others for ages apparently

I hope all our plans will straighten out soon as they have dragged on such ages.

Yr loving

H Talbot

I addressed my letters to B to Hotel du Nord. Milan.

That was the last of the Talbot letters to survive from World War 1. It seems likely that Humphrey did finally join up with Bridget, and that they saw out the war together in Italy.

In the spring of 1918 Germany withdrew her forces from the Italian conflict to prepare for a Spring Offensive on the Western Front. Even so it was not until October 1918 that Italy, which had suffered such huge losses, felt it had enough soldiers to launch an offensive. The attack targeted Vittorio Veneto, across the River Piave, and a breakthrough was finally achieved. On the 31st of November three hundred thousand Austrian soldiers surrendered and on that day armistices were signed with both Austria and Hungary, no longer united since the overthrow of the Habsburg Monarchy and the collapse of the Austro-Hungarian Empire.

Bridget remained in Italy until some time in 1919. For her work at the Italian front, Bridget Elizabeth Talbot was awarded the Italian Medal for Valour, the Croce di Guerra. A return to the quiet of Little Gaddesden however held little appeal for 'General' Talbot. She would soon seek to continue wartime work elsewhere.

Did Kathleen finally join up with her sister and brother in Italy? It seems not, but she did leave Clopton and cross the Channel. Red Cross archives reveal that on the 16th of January 1918 Kathleen began nursing at the B.R.C.S. hospital in France. She then moved on to the No 1 Anglo Belge Hospital and the Gourmoyen Bray Hospital, before being discharged on the 16th of April, 1919. K. kept one more document about Clopton, a menu.

On Tuesday 18th November, 1919, the First Annual Dinner of Clopton War Hospital was held at the Restaurant Frascati, Oxford St in London.

After dining on a six course meal which include Filet de Sole Fleury a l'Ancienne and Poulet roti Boulangere, twenty eight people signed Kathleen's card, including Odeyne Hodgson and C. Liddell.

Chapter 22

Aftermath

On the 3rd September, 1914, as he contemplated the outbreak of war, the British Foreign Secretary, Lord Grey of Falloden, wrote, 'The lamps are going out all over Europe; we shall not see them lit again in our lifetime'.

Just over four bloody years later, when the conflict in Western Europe was over, only a handful of lights went on at Ashridge.

Following the death of his wife in 1917, Earl Brownlow had retreated to Belton, where he was to die four years later and much of Ashridge House was shut up. There was now only a skeleton staff to look after the estate and gardens and at Little Gaddesden House there were three Talbots where there had been six.

In November, 1918, Humphrey was now thirty five, Bridget almost thirty four and Kathleen only twenty five. The future looked bleak.

There were still shortages of food, widespread unemployment, and the promised 'homes fit for heroes' were not being built. Many in the upper classes feared a communist revolution was likely in Britain, two years after one had been successful in Russia. Death duties were crippling many in the aristocracy and some of the great estates were being sold off and their great houses pulled down. Many army officers, like General Philip Wheatley, the son of Colonel Wheatley of the Manor House, left to become farmers in East Africa.

The Talbots' golden Victorian and Edwardian past was well and truly buried and Little Gaddesden must have been a melancholy place to which to return. They would visit Geoffrey's grave of course and that of their parents, and think of the young boys from the scouts and the brass band who had been killed in what was supposed to be 'the War to end all Wars'. What were they to do with the rest of their lives?

Chapter 23

Humphrey – A Startling Announcement

Humphrey often suffered from depression and he seems to have been happiest in helping protect the past. He would try and preserve what he could, not least the gardens of Ashridge House, and he began the Ashridge Flower Shows and 'took upon himself much of the organizing and supervisory work'. He was not short of money. As someone of 'independent means' he had access to considerable funds and of course had many rich relatives. However he did decide to give up the lease of the Talbots' London home at 28, Cadogan Gardens, that was finally surrendered in 1919. In the immediate post war period he seems to have divided his time between Little Gaddesden House and the (*very Conservative)* Carlton Club in London, and looked as if he would be a life long bachelor. But it appears that he was something of a dark horse, though an unlucky one.

On Dec 18th, 1920, this startling announcement appeared in the Times:-

'The marriage arranged between Mr. Humphrey.J.Talbot and Miss Jacynth Ellerton will not take place'.

(A mere four months later Ms Ellerton married Guy Douglas Hamilton Warrack in the Lady Chapel in Winchester Cathedral. Had H been two timed?)

Miss Ellerton had just turned twenty two when the engagement was broken off and was fifteen years younger than H. She was the daughter of a clergyman from Cheshire and seems to have been working as a book illustrator. Ms Ellerton seems to have been somewhat profligate with her affections. She was married a total of three times and divorced twice, ending up as Lady Lawrence, wife of the diplomat and writer Sir John Waldemar Lawrence, Editor of Frontline Magazine and an influential lay member of the Church of England. By her second marriage she had a son, Hugh Hudson, the director of the award winning film, 'Chariots of Fire'. She died just before her ninetieth birthday.

We don't know who was responsible for breaking off the engagement. A comment by Phil Wheatley of the Manor House *(see later)* suggests it could have been H, but it must have been a deeply bruising experience all the same. However Humphrey was surrounded by beauty, both natural and man made.

His obituary in the Times said:-

'... from his earliest childhood he acquired a love of all things beautiful: both from his parents and from his aunt, Lady Brownlow, whose home at Ashridge was a political and artistic rendezvous. In course of time he inherited from them- as well as from his aunts Lady Pembroke and Lady Lowthian, many works of art and pictures (notably Watts 'Rider of the White Horse' and 'Hope') ....Humphrey Talbot had a discerning eye and in unexpected places often rescued rarities ranging from china and glassware ducks to children's toys'.

After his formal discharge from the army with the rank of acting Captain, a title he used, and his failed romance, he spent much of his time, as we've mentioned, trying to look after the gardens at Ashridge House and trying to prevent the destruction of all he so loved. It is due to him that the beautiful old early Jacobean house of Swakeleys near Uxbridge in Middlesex was saved. In 1921, as its estate was being broken up and sold in lots for building new houses, he intervened and bought the house and the immediate parkland. That prevented its destruction, but Humphrey could not afford the costs of refurbishment. The roof was caving in and there was dry rot throughout the house. So, in 1927, after some initial refurbishment, he sold Swakeleys to the sports association of the Foreign Office with the condition that he retained the first, quite magnificent, floor as a tenant. 'Here he arranged an exquisite collection of furniture and pictures', said his obituary in the Gazette, '.... and entertained many hundreds of visitors from the Dominions and historical societies as well as other guests. The garden he made there was known to be one of the most beautiful in England. Queen Mary visited Swakeleys in 1926'.

Humphrey lived on there until the Second World War, helping the building to survive further crises with the help of the Society for the Preservation of Ancient Buildings, of which he became Vice Chairman. It was said of him that 'he knew every bit of good architecture in every corner of England'. Swakeleys House and grounds are still there today, occasionally open to the public. It is no mean memorial, though the gardens are a shadow of their former selves.

As one might expect, the restless, independent, Bridget did not stay at home for long. She had loved the responsibility she had been given, or more likely taken, when nursing on the Italian front, but after the war ended the wounded were sent to Italian hospitals and she had to look further afield for action. She found it in Turkey.

Following the Bolshevik revolution in Russia in 1917 civil war had broken out. Some of those in the former Imperial Army had joined the so called 'White' forces fighting the 'Reds'. Despite receiving aid from Britain and others in the West, they were gradually driven back and in November 1920 a White Army under General Wrangel was surrounded in the Crimea. The Allies *(USA, UK and France)* sent around one hundred steamers and other vessels to Sevastopol to help General Wrangel evacuate his army. The last steamer left Crimea on the 26th November. As soon as the Bolsheviks entered Sevastopol that day it was reported that they shot all the dock workers who had helped with the evacuation.

The convoys sailed for Istanbul (*Constantinople)* but were not allowed to land officially for health reasons. One group was then sent to Gallipoli and another to the island of Lemnos. A third stayed in the vicinity of Istanbul.

Estimates vary about the number of refugees. A semi-official figure says that one hundred and forty six thousand, two hundred, Russians, including twenty nine thousand civilians, were evacuated. Some had cholera and typhus.

Lady Muriel Paget was among the philanthropists who rushed to help and it was perhaps due to her that Bridget went to the Touzla refugee camp near Istanbul to work.

Bridget's experience in wartime Italy would have made her an obvious choice to go, but it required considerable courage to head for a camp where disease was rampant. She remained in Turkey from 1920 to 1922, setting up a committee to deal with the Russian refugees and later a co-operative farm colony in Asia Minor. She was awarded an OBE for her work.

Having returned form nursing in France and Belgium, Kathleen seems to have remained at Little Gaddesden, developing her musical interests, producing musical plays and masques for local societies. In June 1920 The Times announced that her aunt 'The Hon. Mrs. Carpenter (widow of the Admiral) will give a small dance for her nieces Miss Kathleen Talbot and Miss Avis Hodgson', which was a way of saying that they were eligible, but after the carnage of the war there were many fewer suitable men available. No engagements resulted.

Chapter 24

The Sale Of Ashridge

Then, in 1923, came news from Belton that the new Lord Brownlow, a fourth cousin of Uncle Addy, who had died two years before, was going ahead with the sale of the Ashridge estate to pay death duties. In doing so he was following the instructions contained in the will of his predecessor. Even so it was a considerable shock. Ashridge was a prime site for developers, close to London, with a railway station just three miles away. Just the place for a golf course or two and some superior urban villas. The villagers, almost all of whom were Brownlow tenants, feared for the future.

The Talbot children were of course tenants as well. Little Gaddesden House belonged to the Ashridge estate, as did the Manor House where Colonel Wheatley lay dying, having lost his daughter, his Angel, the year before. There was a reassuring ray of light-Humphrey had been appointed one of the three Trustees giving the responsibility of selling off the estate. *(The two others were Brownlow Tower and Lionel Cust.)*
Some years later Bridget composed a not entirely objective account of the events that followed. Writing of her brother she said 'he continually urged his co-trustees to sell off the estate themselves and so save the lovely park from destruction by gambling speculators. The other two trustees were old and unwilling to have the bother and preferred to sell to the highest speculative bidder.
If the trustees had sold direct and not through the middle man profiteer, thousands of pounds would have been saved for the estate and the most beautiful park in England saved.
During these years my brother had (with little expense) so arranged the garden with skill and artistic colouring- that people

came from all parts of the country to see it. Formerly there had been twenty gardeners to run it and then there were five'.

In 1924 Bridget and Humphrey did in fact help save part of the Ashridge grounds, including the Golden Valley, as we will see, but her narrative leaps ahead to the fate of Ashridge House itself.

'When, later, the Conservatives took over (*the party bought the House as a political college in 1928)* the garden was allowed to lose its beauty of colour and arrangement. The gate money went down to a very small amount.

After the speculator bought the house and estate, I heard that the house was to be sold off separately. I at once got all the particulars together and thought out a plan of action. My idea was to have Ashridge as an Empire or Commonwealth College club where people coming from the Dominions could come on arrival and meet members of the Government and others. A place where there could be lectures and discussions on subjects such as defence, emigration, agriculture, shipping etc. Empire politicians could visit and lecture from time to time. My idea was that each Dominion should own a bit of the park and that individuals should each save a tree and have their name attached thereto. This scheme would have saved one of the most beautiful parks in England. The Home Farm and land, I planned, should be used as a land training settlement for the unemployed. The unemployed would then be in direct touch with Dominion visitors and British politicians. The latter seemed curiously incapable of realising the demoralising effect of the dole and its future effect on the morale of the nation'.

According to Bridget she was then betrayed by the architect she had consulted, Clough Williams Ellis who, though sworn to secrecy, told the local MP (the Chairman of the Conservative Party) Mr. J.C.C Davidson about her plan.

'Mr. Davidson at once took to the idea, and turned the scheme into a party college on which he would have a controlling influence. He would have a comfortable residence in his constituency and the good old stables for his hunters. I did not know my scheme had been given away. Our MP had all the strings to pull in his hands. Being a personal friend of Mr. Baldwin *(the then Conservative Prime Minister)* he could offer a peerage to Mr. Broughton for the fund with which to buy the house. Eventually I was informed that the house was to come on the market *(This must have been in late 1927 or early 1928).*

At the time I was busy organising a large pageant of Queen Elizabeth's visit to Ashridge. Over three hundred people were taking part including Coldstream Guards dressed as Beefeaters, many horses and ponies, and even a live camel on which the Persian Ambassador rode.

It was the last swan song of Ashridge of the old days. The garden was looking quite lovely with a blaze of rhododendrons on either side as a brilliant procession made its way down the lawn.

Halfway down the lawn the Paulonia tree was covered with purple flowers- a most unusual sight. The Chapel bells rang and guns were let off. Two hundred gaily dressed country dancers lined the route'.

In this article, written during the Second World War, Bridget is full of anger and contempt for the 'disastrous Conservative government', and its failure to back her vision for the house and the estate:-

'It was the same criminal neglect and disastrous lack of vision which led to the present disaster of war'.

She went on 'The country people who had lived there for generations, were turned out of their cottages by the wholesale gambling speculators. Rich retired civil servants and city merchants bought up 'modernised' cottages at fabulous prices and turned them into weekend residences............. The hideous and false name of Conservative had settled like a blight on this structure of Ashridge.

The Conservatives could not and would not save the beautiful park or the cottages or the good farm lands. This rich farm land lay derelict and weedy for years labelled 'Ripe for development', spreading weeds on the adjoining county'.

There is much more of this, and Bridget wrote later that, on hearing the house was to become a Conservative College, 'I at once left the Conservative Party'. *(One doubts if she was still a member by that time)*. It is no surprise that Bridget subsequently joined the National Labour Party under Ramsay MacDonald, an unusual thing for a woman of her class to do. National Labour was the rump of the Labour Party which had followed Prime Minister MacDonald into a coalition with the Conservatives during the Great Depression. It was far from being socialist, and soon withered away, a bit like the SDP in later years. While Bridget could not be called a left winger she was proud to say she was anti-Conservative.

However Bridget's account of the break up of Ashridge is rather sweeping, and in parts, inaccurate. The magnificent Ashridge House is now a management college and superbly maintained. Although there has been additional building it has been done discreetly. The great staircase and grand reception rooms would still be easily recognized by the Brownlows and Talbots today.

Also, in 1923, some of the local villagers were able to buy their cottages at reasonable prices and anyone who comes to the Ashridge Estate and Little Gaddesden today can see how much of beauty has been saved *(Although they can also see, on Nettleden Road, some houses designed by Clough Williams Ellis and with the initials JCCD(avidson) inscribed on them. These cannot be described as the architect's finest work.)*

However, if Ashridge House had been 'lost', first to speculators in 1924 and then to the Tory party four years later, there was still much of the park to be saved, so Bridget set to work. Her first intervention related to the Golden Valley and some other parts of the estate and the great beechwoods.

In her book 'Bounteous Days' her cousin Conty *(Talbot)* Sitwell reproduced part of her diaries for the period which gives a vivid picture of Bridget in action:-

Ashridge, October, 1925
I went to stay at Little Gaddesden with Bridget.
The next day history was made, as far as saving the park at Ashridge was concerned; a plot was hatched to preserve it. For it

was to be sold and all the marvellous beeches were to be cut down and sold.

It was a Sunday and Bridget and I walked to church in the morning. I went and looked at father's grave; also at Geoffrey's, who had been killed flying in the war....

In the afternoon we two walked up to Ashridge by the familiar little paths. It really looked marvellous — the green slopes lying so peacefully in the sun — more beautiful than ever, now that we thought it might perish with all its memories and all that it meant to us and to many others.

When we got home again and were beginning tea Jim Craufurd *(a barrister from nearby Aldbury)* appeared. A plan to save the park was discussed and our talks continued until 10pm. We went to church in the middle of it and the choir sang 'Jerusalem' and the words 'England's green and pleasant land' spurred us on still further. So we rang Humphrey who was a Trustee for the estate, and asked him to meet us in London the next day to discuss a joint campaign. Jim and I composed a letter which we hoped would be signed by the Prime Minister, Mr. Baldwin, and Lord Balfour, to be sent to The Times.

October 12th

The next day was most exciting, in one way or another. Bridget and I set off early for Berkhamsted, just catching the train, and were met by Humphrey at Euston as planned. I did respect him, for he looked quite ill with worry and unhappiness over Ashridge. I felt how deeply he loved beauty and realised its tremendous importance. We held a long discussion, feeling like conspirators, and then launched Bridget off to Downing St. to do what she could.

I went back to Marchmont *(her childhood home)* in the evening and Bridget rang up to say that she had caught Mr. Baldwin, who was most anxious to help and had wired Lord Balfour to this effect. I did admire her determination and felt she should have a statue put up to her as the Saviour of Ashridge. Humphrey also rang up and asked if I would try to get hold of the Archbishop, a connection of Willie's *(her husband)* to join the appeal; but I flunked it.

October 13th

The Times could almost have been called an Ashridge number, for there were a leading article, appeals, letters, and comments about

Mr. Baldwin's interview. Indeed the first item of Home News was that Lord Balfour had called upon Mr. Baldwin yesterday.

October 14th

There were still columns in The Times about it all; but it was still rather a painful subject really with so little time to act and so much beauty threatened. We were very amused by the leading article, appealing to Humphrey (as one of the Trustees) who, having been something of a family joke for years, was now the centre of so much attention.

The campaign, which Bridget spearheaded, and to which she made a substantial financial contribution via the public subscription fund, secured much land for the National Trust. £40,000 was raised which allowed the Trust to acquire its first extensive tract of standing timber.

Bridget wrote, 'George Trevelyan carried on the campaign to raise money, Miss Courtauld gave vast sums and Duncombe Terrace and miles of Comb Wood and the Downs were saved. Alas there was not enough to save this most beautiful park in England. It can now only be compared to Muswell Hill and Ealing'. Bridget wrote that in 1961 and one can only conclude that by then her eyesight was failing. The National Trust has continued to this day the programme of purchasing in the area, initiated by her.

However, to be fair to Bridget, in 1930 there were further efforts to sell of parts of the estate, some successful, as can be seen in some of the drives by the entrance to Ashridge Golf Course. Once more the redoubtable Miss Talbot swung into action, again with a large measure of success.

It cannot be said that Bridget alone saved Ashridge Park but she did more than anyone to preserve the beauty that surrounds the house. She herself claimed, in her Who's Who entry, that she was 'Instrumental in securing Ashridge Estate to National Trust'. Today it is evident that her worst fears have not been realised.

The house is now the much admired Ashridge Management College with students from around the world, including the former Dominions. Large sums of money have been ploughed into repairing the fabric and the gardens are once more immaculate. The house is surrounded by miles of the most beautiful land in England, enjoyed by tens of thousands each year who can easily get lost in the gorgeous woodland and catch a glimpse of the deer whose ancestors first came to Ashridge almost a thousand years ago. Red Kites wheel overhead, rare cattle and sheep graze nearby, and the unobtrusive golf course pavilion is skillfully designed to fit in with the landscape. There is no statue to Bridget but the National Trust has put up a plaque at its centre near the Bridgewater monument, recognising her outstanding contribution to saving the Estate.

And, by the late 1920's Little Gaddesden House was safely in Talbot hands. Bridget was to live there for the rest of her life.

However there is another, perhaps murkier, episode involving the Talbots and the break up of the Ashridge Estate, though the main accuser is a far from disinterested figure, the son of the Agent, Colonel William Wheatley, who lived in the Manor House.

General Phil Wheatley wrote his autobiography in 1934, the year before his death. He had moved to what is now Kenya shortly after the war to try his hand at farming. He was not very successful, but he had been a key figure in the Settler's Revolt in 1923 which took place shortly after he arrived there. It was aimed at preventing black Africans gaining significant political rights, but was put down by a cousin of Wheatley, Lord Lytton, who said he was quite prepared to shoot him if necessary. The revolt then fizzled out.

Subsequently the General founded the Nanyuki cottage hospital and was responsible for the erection of the town's race course and polo ground. He was, in many ways, a model retired soldier, but he was, at least in early life, a racist, writing of two Cabinet members as 'unspeakable Jews', and saying that 'the average white man abominates the Somali and the Indian.' Reflecting on a visit to Germany, which he had made in 1910, Phil Wheatley said, 'I came to the conclusion that year that the average German mind is like a cess-pit and nothing that I saw or read in after years altered my opinion in the least'. He did acknowledge, however, that he had 'a hasty temper', which he fought to curb.

The historian C.J. Duddon wrote of the General's time in the Raj that 'Wheatley shared, and indeed could be said to exemplify, the prejudices of.... the most bigoted members of the Anglo-Indian Community'.

However Phil Wheatley undoubtedly loved his 'Dear old Dad', which is how he addressed his weekly letters to his father back in Little Gaddesden and he was outraged by the way he had been treated..

'Too true, he was extremely badly treated by the old *(Earl)* Brownlow who left my father without any kind of pension or legacy after thirty years service'.

He had no time for the Earl.

'Lord Brownlow inherited massive sums and frittered it away. He was a champion waster and never did anything worthwhile in his life'.

Wheatley's attitude to Lady Adelaide was very different.

'She was a perfect dear and I loved her from the first moment I met her to her death during the War'.

Perhaps Phil Wheatley felt a little guilty about money because his father and uncle had bailed him out of financial difficulty several times in the past, but he was also aware of how painful his father's last years had been.

'My father was taken ill with bladder trouble in December 1907. Though he lived for nearly sixteen years afterwards he was never the same man again. He was often in ghastly pain but he still carried on always like the gallant undaunted fellow that he was'. In addition the Colonel had seen his daughter Angelica Pamela, always known as Angel, the childhood friend of K who had worked as a nurse at Hemel Hempstead hospital, die of a painful illness in 1922, aged just twenty eight.

There is no doubt that the Colonel, known as Nep, had been an outstanding Agent, but now, after Earl Brownlow's death, Phil Wheatley says that his ailing father had to write an account of his stewardship of the estate for the Trustees, justifying his decisions, and accounting for expenditure. It was humiliating.

Then the Trustees decided to sell the Manor House, the Wheatleys' home.

'The last Earl Brownlow, who died in 1921, behaved disgracefully to my father. They had been together for thirty eight years and my father had married a Cust, *(a relative of the Brownlows)* yet his house was to be sold over his head and he was to be turned out on to the village green. A handsome reward for thirty eight years of loyal and priceless service in many difficult times'. Phil then turned his fire on the Trustees and in particular Humphrey Talbot. He claims that H's uncle, General Sir Reggie Talbot, refused to allow Humphrey in the house because of how he had behaved to a girl to whom he was engaged. *(Presumably Jacynth Ellerton.)* 'Humphrey Talbot always a nasty piece of work. His father and mother were such nice people as was his brother Geoffrey who was killed in the war'.

How much of this should we believe? Phil Wheatley's half sister Pearl described his autobiography as 'terribly pathetic'. 'Poor Phil was desperately lonely out in Kenya as he hated leaving my father, whom he adored'. And the incident with Uncle Reggie? Well it did not stop Humphrey being appointed as one of the executors and beneficiaries of his uncle's and aunt's estates and having dinner with them on many occasions subsequently.

However the Trustees were intent on selling the Wheatleys' home, though fortunately the Colonel died shortly before they did so. The carpenters on the Ashridge Estate he had managed for so long made the coffin and followed the hearse for the cremation at Golders Green. His ashes were brought back to Little Gaddesden and laid on the grave of his daughter. Shortly after, in 1924, the Manor House and some surrounding property were purchased - by a relative of one of the Trustees, none other than Humphrey Talbot's sister, Kathleen.

She paid £6,000 for it and two adjoining cottages and land. Mrs. Wheatley and her two surviving daughters, Pearl and Prudence moved out.

This does not look good, but perhaps the daughters, now grown up, were already living elsewhere, and later that year the late

Colonel's wife, a Cust, was at Belton, so the family was looking after her. *(She died in Hampstead in 1932.)*

And it should be pointed out that one of the other trustees, Lionel Cust, who had to agree to the sale, was also one of her relatives. Would he have been party to her being thrown out? Lionel Cust implicitly denied that the sale had been rigged in Kathleen Talbot's favour.

In a letter, agreeing with Humphrey that the portrait of Elizabeth 1st in the Manor House, which had been painted on a door, should be regarded as a fixture, Lionel wrote, 'I have no concern as to whom may be the Purchaser of this house.'

Finally, in 1931 the Colonel's daughter Prudence Wheatley and her husband, Captain Marston Buzzard, stayed overnight at the Manor House as guests of Kathleen Talbot, so if there were hard feelings they seem to have softened by then.

Even so there does, at the very least, seem to have been a potential conflict of interest over the sale.

From now onwards the three Talbot children had their own homes, Humphrey at Swakeleys, Bridget at Little Gaddesden House and Kathleen at the Manor House in Little Gaddesden.

K kept a visitors' book and it reveals that H was a frequent guest, but increasingly the children, now moving into middle age, began to live more separate lives. No-one remembers Bridget and Kathleen spending much time together in subsequent years. Their temperaments were certainly very different.

Chapter 25

Later Lives

Kathleen

Before she had moved into the Manor House, Kathleen had begun developing her musical career. She started the West Herts music festival in Berkhamsted which lasted until 1939. She conducted the Little Gaddesden Choir.

She produced performances of Arne's setting of Milton's Masque of Comus, the manuscript of which was said to have been left at the old Ashridge House. The first performance was in 1922 and in her book of memories of the Ashridge Estate Doris Fenn remembered taking part:-

'The stage was the gardens and sloping lawns of Little Gaddesden House'. With other schoolgirls Doris acted as 'Water Nymphs dressed in flowing muslin which had been dyed in various pale colours. Uncle played the violin and some villagers joined in singing with Miss Talbot's guests'.

The novelist and historian Peter Quenell also took part, and there are photographs of the event in 'Little Gaddesden-A Century Remembered', published by the Rural Heritage Society.

There was an even grander performance at Eton College on 11th December 1922, with John Gielgud as the 'Younger Brother'. Heady stuff for a young woman producer not yet thirty. Kathleen may have been thought quiet but she was clearly very determined and confident.

In 1924, as we have seen, K moved into the Manor House and she continued to produce masques, including one in June of that year at the Old Palace in Hatfield. It was by Thomas Campion, and in it she cast some of her friends including Mr. and Mrs. Granville Ram and Miss Ruth Blezard, a friend of Humphrey's *(and remembered decades later in his will)*. The masque was produced for the benefit of the Hertfordshire County Nursing Association.

On August 7th, 1924 Kathleen Talbot was Mistress of the Revels at the Elizabethan Fair at Upton Pyne House and the following year dipped her toe into local politics, standing as an independent, in the County Council elections. She lost and does not appear to have repeated the experience.

Later in 1925, now in her early thirties, K decided to travel. Presumably, after inheriting from her parents and from the Brownlows, she had money over from the purchase of her new home and wished to see the world, and perhaps find a life's companion.

Her companions on this journey were to be her relatives and old wartime nursing colleagues, Avis Hodgson and her mother Odeyne, together with Avis's father, the Reverend Francis Henry Hodgson, who had officiated at Geoffrey's funeral.

K booked with the Rotterdam Lloyd Royal Mail Line. 'The Direct Route to Sumatra and Java'. She sailed from Southampton to Batavia on the 17th November, 1925, sharing with Mavis a second class cabin no. 78/9 on the SS Insulinde. The company was keen to point out that, 'You will see from the enclosed plan that this room is an excellent position on the port side of the 'B' deck'. After spending a few days in Java they left Sourabaya on the 22nd December on the SS Houtman bound for Sydney. 'If you prefer you could of course disembark at Brisbane, but we are afraid that the following steamer for Sydney will not be leaving until a month later'.

On the 10th of February, 1926 they left Sydney on SS Maloja bound for Marseilles.

K does not seem to have met a suitable young man. She and Avis remained close friends, indeed Avis's is the first name in Kathleen's Visitors Book for the Manor House, showing she stayed there between Nov 1st and 3rd 1924.

Constance(*Cooie*), Lane is the second. Avis and her mother Odeyne stayed regularly with K until at least 1934, when entries in the book stopped, resuming in the 1950s.

Unlike K, Avis did marry. She was in her late thirties when she became the wife of the Rev. Francis Edward Spurway, a clergyman like her father, and had a daughter.

(When K died Avis and her daughter attended the funeral and were remembered in her will. Avis died in 1988 aged ninety.)
But by the early 1930's another woman had entered K's life and would one day inherit her home, Dorothy Agnes Alice Erhar*(d)*t Mus.B

Dorothy Erhart's name first appears in the Manor House visitors' book in 1931, showing she stayed there on Feb 16th and 17th. She was back on the 23rd of that month, then in March, in April and in May. *(K then went off to produce the Weymouth Amateurs in the musical comedy 'The Quaker Girl').* Dorothy was back in July, November and December.
The next year she appears to have been in semi-permanent residence. Sometimes these visits were directly related to musical events, a Wayfarer's Concert in December 1932 for example, and then a Conductors' School in February, 1933.
Dorothy Erhart was a harpsichordist, a somewhat rare creature in those days, and also conducted. She founded 'The Erhart Chamber Orchestra'(Leader David Martin) in 1926, ('For terms and vacant dates apply to; The Imperial Concert Agency, 20 Kingly Street, London W1 Regent 1140') and also 'The Erhart Ensemble', other members of which were Donald Munro, Baritone, and Edith Lake, Viola da Gamba.
'The Erhart Ensemble' was formed 'for the purpose of presenting music of the 17th and 18th centuries — not only works by the great masters, such as Bach and Handel, but also music by lesser known composers, which may have been undeservedly forgotten or neglected'.
According to Barbara Cassell, both Dorothy and her mother came to live at the Manor House.
Does all this suggest that K and Dorothy were a loving couple? It is possible, but more likely that these were two early middle aged women, both passionate about music, who preferred living with a companion than living alone and who became very good friends. They were to stay together until parted by death.

On Feb 3rd 1936 in an army hut in Little Gaddesden a production of 'Orpheus' opened. The chorus was trained by the now forty two year old Kathleen and the performance was conducted by Dorothy. Also that year they wrote 'Spare Time Music' for the BBC, which included penny whistles and mouth organs. One of their broadcasts, on Thursday 21 April, 1936, was entitled 'Yorkshire Pudding'.

K had become a passionate advocate of music in public life.

In 1934 the Oxford University Press published 'Village Music — Some suggestions for conductors and organisers', by Kathleen Talbot. K had gone to some considerable effort to ensure it was taken seriously. She had it endorsed by The British Federation of Musical Competition Festivals, the Joint Committee for Music and Drama in Villages, the National Federation of Women's Institutes, the School of English Church Music, the Free Church Choir Union, the Church Music Society, the Pipers' Guild, the English Folk Dance and Song Society, the Hertfordshire Rural Music School and the Chamber Music Association. The booklet opens with a resounding statement. 'Choral singing is probably the most perfect form of social recreation that can be found today. It provides a complete change from the routine of ordinary life and has amazing power of developing the imagination and a love of beauty'...

The book is full of practical advice. 'Now the first step towards making music in a village is to find a leader'. Such a person would need to possess a –'good temper and unlimited patience'. They would face an uphill task as '.... the singing and playing in country places of worship is probably worse than in any other branch of music today'... Was she thinking of Little Gaddesden?

Warming to her theme, in 1935 she wrote twice to The Times, in August about 'Amateur Musicians – Reasons for their Disappearance' and in September about 'Education in Music – help for the Amateur'. In October, 1936, she spoke at the British Federation of Music Competition Festivals about 'the difficulties in finding the right type of music for girl guides.' By 1937 she was the Secretary of the Mid. and West Herts. Festival held in Berkhamsted.

K was also developing a considerable reputation as a cook. In December 1933 she published 'The Epicure's Monthly Companion', full of original cookery recipes for each month of the year. *(It also contained a poem by Kathleen.)* This gastronomical guide included recipes for Andalusian Gaspacho and Strawberry Fritters and had a recipe for mincemeat devised in the 1750's by an ancestor, Lady Walsingham. However most of the recipes are French and in the book K expressed her thanks for the advice of Mme. Marguerite Thevenin and M. Henri Thevenin. The introduction was by a former diplomat, Sir Stephen Gaselee. K assumed a considerable knowledge of French among her readers. *(The book was republished, unaltered, in 1952).*

By 1939, now approaching forty six, K had become the music convener of the London Council of the Guild of Townswomen's Music and Drama Festivals. *(It surely had an acronym).*
It is frustrating for a biographer to find relatively little evidence of what the subject really felt. K was modest about her achievements, left no diary and few letters that we can trace, but at this 1939 event she was reported as making a heartfelt plea.
'She said that the study and practice of music and drama was a valuable help to steady the nerves, and help them to preserve a sense of balance, beauty and imagination. In keeping alive these arts you are taking a very great part in preserving the moral and physical health of the nation at the present time'.
The present time was of course the onset of yet another World War. When K wrote to The Times in 1940 saying that 'women long to take part in the country's defence' she was undoubtedly thinking of herself as well.

Bridget

In the 1930's it seems that Bridget spent a great deal of her time away from Little Gaddesden. As she moved into her late forties her appetite for action did not seem to have diminished.
She went to Russia in 1932 with Lady Muriel Paget's Mission.

Lady Muriel was the elder of two daughters of the Earl of Winchelsea and educated privately at home. She married, had five children, helped set up the 'Invalid Kitchens of London' movement and in 1915, when her youngest child was only a few months old, set of for Petrograd, where she and her friend Lady Sibyl Grey, with the support of the Empress Alexandra Feodorovna, set up an Anglo-Russian hospital for the treatment of wounded soldiers. The following year Lady Muriel set up a number of field hospitals and food kitchens in the Ukraine. She was there in 1918 when she had to be evacuated as the Bolsheviks advanced. Despite this she returned to Russia the following year and was allowed by the Communists to continue her charitable work. She had few illusions about them but focused on practical schemes which would help the needy all over Eastern Europe. Bridget had met her in London after the evacuation of the 'White' Russians from the Crimea to Turkey.

In 1932 Lady Muriel's particular concern was the DBSs, the Displaced British Subjects in the USSR.

They were a relatively small number of British residents in the Soviet Union who were unable (for example, because of age or infirmity or poverty) or, in a few cases, had been unwilling to leave Russia after the October Revolution of 1917. Many were tainted by association with the old Tsarist regime and had become highly vulnerable, even though they might have married into Russian families or (in certain circumstances) have been born and brought up in Russia and spoke little or no English at all.

It was these people that Lady Muriel wanted Bridget Talbot to assist her in helping. The British Subjects in Russia Relief Organisation was set up in Britain, a flat bought in Moscow, and a dacha was eventually built at Detsoye Selo. The small country house was intended to serve as a retirement and convalescent home. It opened in 1933 and was placed under the supervision of a Mrs. Morley.

In 1938 there were allegations, made under privilege in the House of Commons by the left wing MP 'Red' Ellen Wilkinson and subsequently officially denied, that Lady Muriel had worked for the British Intelligence Services. The dacha was subsequently closed.

Was Bridget also a spy?

This is most unlikely. True she was a passionate patriot, but she had a jaundiced eye for much of the British establishment, which she had seen at such close quarters. She was already moving left and had joined the National Labour Party in Britain in 1931, helping Ramsay MacDonald in the election campaign.

Lady Muriel's outstanding relief work for so many over so long leaves no doubt that her main driving force was compassion for those in need.

Lady Muriel Paget died of cancer, aged sixty, a great and now hardly remembered philanthropist and humanitarian relief worker. Bridget was one of those at her memorial service.

It looks as though Bridget was just the sort of person you would want to barge through bureaucratic obstruction, be it capitalist or communist, and work all hours to achieve a socially just objective. However it is unlikely that you would want her to run an organisation for long. We suspect she would have got a little bored and restless and tact may not have been her strongest suit. For a passionate democrat she was a bit of a dictator.

Throughout the inter war years Bridget kept up a constant stream of letters to The Times about local and national issues. On December 23rd,1929 she wrote in aid of a fund set up to save the village green at Little Gaddesden and arranged the production of a sixteenth century play, 'Gammer Gurton's Needle' by the LG players in the Barn theatre in the village. Constance Lane painted the scenery. In December 1930 as the Great Depression settled in she wrote about 'Settlement in Dominions' and was not shy about proclaiming her own achievements:-

'Some years ago, when the White Russian Army was broken up and thousands of refugees came to Turkey I started a farm colony on some waste land in Asia Minor. We had only a small amount of capital, but within two years those Russians had not only become self supporting but had made enough money either to pay back the original capital or to go and make a fresh start in the Balkans when Kemal's troops swept the country. The others who had lived on what charity they could get were not only starving and in bad health but also utterly demoralized'.

Bridget argued that the British government should copy that scheme and send those unemployed to the Dominions with cash loans.

In April 1932 she was writing about the threat to the 'Beauties of Ashridge – the Golden Valley Trees' and had persuaded the historian G.M.Trevelyan, who lived in Berkhamsted and Lords Salisbury, Desborough and Hampden, to be co-signatories. How could one say no to Bridget?

She returned to the issue of unemployment in a letter to the newspaper dated the 9th June, 1933 and headed 'Camp for Unemployed Lads' – 'It is quite certain that unless rapid steps are taken to insist on some compulsory occupation or service in return for the dole the demoralization of the unemployed will be past caring'. She included a detailed costing of her scheme, which was doubtless optimistic given her difficulty with figures. She went on 'After a few years a carefully selected number could be chosen for self-supporting settlement on the land at home or in the Dominions with a repayment of capital'.

In 1937 Bridget, as a member of the National Labour Council was arguing for good conditions for domestic servants and that councils should have first refusal on the sale of farm workers' cottages to stop workers being priced out of their villages, a measure that would have considerable support today in the countryside.

As she approached fifty, B's taste for adventure was undiminished. She states, in 'Who's Who', that in 1937 she sailed on the four-masted sailing ship Pamir to Finland. We are obviously meant to be impressed.

By the 1950's she was making election speeches in which she said she had 'served before the mast in a windjammer and nearly lost her life in a gale off Scandinavia'. The Pamir was a four-masted barque, built in Hamburg in 1905, with 40,900 feet of sails. She was the last commercial sailing ship to round Cape Horn, in 1949. She was used initially in the South American nitrate trade, but in 1931 was sold to the Finnish shipping company of Gustaf Erikson, which used her in the Australian wheat trade. Bridget was crewing on the leg from Cork to Finland when she 'nearly lost her life in a gale'.

(In 1957 most of the Pamir's crew did lose their lives when the ship was caught in a hurricane and sank off the Azores. She had a crew of eighty six including fifty two cadets. There were only six survivors.)

It is likely that it was her 'near death experience' that lay behind B's next entry in 'Who's Who'.

'Started the National Labour enquiry into state of Merchant Navy, 1939', and the next, 'Invested 1939, a watertight electric torch for lifeboats and was instrumental in getting these made compulsory for all MN,RAF and RN personnel, and so saved hundreds of lives'.

It is a large claim, but it does seem as if it is justified.

The Western Morning News, on Wednesday, February 28th 1940, a few months into the war and before Churchill became Prime Minister, gave an account of the previous day's debate in the House of Commons about safety at sea. Part of it read as follows:-

'It was left to a woman MP, Miss Eleanor Rathbone, to extract from the Government an assurance that rafts will be supplied to the Merchant Navy and others vessels, writes our Political Correspondent. There were to be other precautions such as steel helmets against enemy gun attacks. In this campaign Miss Rathbone has had the backing of Miss Bridget Talbot who has made a study of these questions.

Miss Talbot, who was at the House last night, is anxious that the rafts shall have attached to them electric torches . . . in watertight cases. Such torches should also be appended to lifebelts'.

It is not difficult to imagine Bridget pigeonholing the parliamentary press to ensure that her scheme was extensively reported. She had already seen to it that her friends in high places were aware of her ideas. Barbara Cassell, a relative, wrote:-

'Early in the 1939 War *(Bridget)* realised that many sailors were losing their lives after being torpedoed despite wearing life jackets. The trouble was they could not be seen in the dark. She asked - or more, likely told - the Admiralty to fit automatic waterproof lights to the jackets, but the Navy closed ranks against attack from a civilian with mysterious statements about 'technical reasons'. Bridget found a local workshop to make a working example of a light and then she sallied forth again, but she relied upon being related to one of the Sea Lords, and went to see him at the Admiralty. Her forcefulness and his rank led to a sea change'.

She may have had help from an even more distinguished source. According to her first cousin, Lord Walsingham, as reported by another relative, Humphrey Chetwynd-Talbot:-

'Bridget telephoned Buckingham Palace to discuss her ideas and asked to be put through to the King! Perhaps typically of the time and of Bridget's forcefulness, she was put through and found herself speaking to George V, (If true, it was surely George VI) 'With his interest in the sea he was readily persuaded that the idea had potential and thereafter things happened'. Mr. Chetwynd-Talbot went on, 'I went to her memorial service in East London.... (in 1971, over twenty five years after the end of the war) ...and it was packed with people who wished to remember'.

Barbara Cassell had another story of 'Bridget at War', which she says B told with a chuckle as well as with indignation. She quotes her as follows:-

'I arrived at Glasgow railway station during the war to see thousands of soldiers settling down for the night on the hard platforms. Naturally I asked what was going on and eventually was told that they were due to embark in a convoy to fight abroad, but that owing to the possibility of air raids they had to stay on land until the last moment. I asked the officer why he didn't find proper billets for the men, but he shrugged his shoulders. So the next day I booked a room in the best hotel and told the Red Cross that the Press were coming and told the Press the Red Cross were coming. We had a meeting and they appointed me to go to the Lord Provost of Glasgow. He was a very bad tempered man who didn't like being told what to do by a Sassenach woman. I told him he could accommodate lots of soldiers in his corridors alone. I said it was monstrous that these men were going abroad to fight for us, where some would die and we were letting them spend their last nights in this country on hard platforms. He gave in and billets were arranged for the men'. Mrs Cassell went on......

'She chuckled when telling this story when she said that the Provost had a heart attack in the next couple of days- and it probably served him right'.

Throughout the war Bridget continued to be concerned about those at sea, and their relatives on land. In 1943 she became a Vice-President of The Watch Ashore, a charity concerned with the welfare of relatives of seamen in the Merchant Navy. Its annual report for 1943 said that Miss Bridget Talbot OBE had become a Vice-President and 'has been one of the most forceful and lively advocates of the watch ever since'.

On November 13th that year she travelled to Newcastle upon Tyne, where she had organised a meeting at the Royal Station Hotel to restart the North East Coastal Branch of the Watch Ashore.

A subsequent report read:

'Miss Bridget Talbot OBE, one of the most dynamic members of the Watch Ashore, was the speaker. She impressed upon the members the fact that constant vigilance was necessary if the Merchant Navy was to get its due. She reminded listeners of the great risks men of the Merchant Navy ran every day in order to keep open our lifeline and stressed the debt those ashore owed to them. Miss Talbot pointed out that the womenfolk of all those connected with the Merchant Navy bore with great fortitude the difficult job of waiting and the anxieties inseparable from the dependants of sailors'.

As one might have expected Bridget became a frequent letter writer to The Times, for example writing on April 22, 1944 on the need for lifeboats on tankers. She had just published what the newspaper described as a 'trenchant little pamphlet' on Empire Transport, priced sixpence. It was 'by that indefatigable worker for the welfare of the Merchant Seamen, Miss Bridget Talbot – urging that post war reorganization of imperial transport services cannot safely be allowed any longer to drift'. B wrote another letter in May calling for an Empire Transport Board. Unfortunately for her, it was published the morning after D Day so would not have been at the forefront of the public's attention over their breakfast table. She was still arguing the case for such a board in January 1948 when, having just celebrated her sixty third birthday she gave an 'at home' on her old sailing ship, Pamir, in the Shadwell Basin of London docks. Bridget also worked continuously for St Dunstan's, a charity set up in 1915 to help blind ex-servicemen. She often had them to tea at her Little Gaddesden home and let camps be held on her land. *(There is a photograph of her at one such camp in 1935 with her cousin, K's wartime colleague, Avis Hodgson, who was a honorary member of the staff of St Dunstans and who, from 1925 to 1939, ran holiday camps for the blinded men.)*

Kathleen

While Bridget obviously loved the limelight it seems as if her younger sister was more reticent. Those who knew her talk of K's private nature and frequent silences, but she appears to have been no less active than her sister during their second World War. However, if Bridget was preoccupied by matters at sea, Kathleen focused on what was happening on the land.

Their father, Alfred Talbot, had started the Little Gaddesden Horticultural Society which was still flourishing and Bridget claimed that in 1914 she had started the cultivation of co-operative gardens on waste land, and that later the Ministry of Agriculture adopted the scheme all over the country. Perhaps so, but in the Second World War, Kathleen was the Talbot who pushed forward these ideas. She travelled the country encouraging people to 'Dig For Victory' and was one of the founders of the Village Produce Association.

In 1942, as a member of the Central Committee of the Home Produce Clubs, K attended a food production conference under the chairmanship of the Duchess of Devonshire, to talk about the organisation's development. She said they wanted nothing less than a Home Produce Club in every village and everyone should try to produce enough for themselves and their families. Food production would be of inestimable value in reducing the need for ships and in feeding the starving countries of the world after the war.

She mentioned a successful experiment which had been tried of villages running their own market stall. People who had been going into town to buy vegetables had supported the idea. Clubs could also arrange for disposal of extra vegetables through co-operative societies. The Duchess of Devonshire said there were now sixty eight Home Produce Clubs in the county but there must be nine hundred villages, which was an indication of the scope for extension of the movement.

As Barbara Cassell noted, 'This (K's work) was not a cushy job for a middle aged lady when one remembers the lack of petrol, black-out and no signposts in most areas and she really did go all over the country'.

She continued her work in the immediate post war years.

By September 1946, Kathleen Talbot, now fifty three and an MBE, had become the national organiser for the Central Committee of the Central County Garden Produce Association (Mm of Ag.)

Also that month she arranged, as honorary organiser, the Village Produce Association Conference.

In August 1947 she attended the Gloucester Home Food Production Society, where she emphasised the importance of growing more dessert apples and soft fruit. She said she could not think of any better war memorials in some of the villages than the planting of some really good apple trees along the village green. Perhaps she was thinking of her brother Geoffrey who had died thirty years before and other friends of her youth.

Humphrey

Whereas Bridget and Kathleen were preoccupied with the present, their elder brother Humphrey seems to have been more at home in the past and helping to preserve what remained of it. Like his two sisters he had not married.

After saving Swakeleys, where he still lived when not at his club, the Carlton, H helped save other old houses and became Vice Chairman of the Society for the Protection of Ancient Buildings. In 1933 he wrote on the society's behalf to protest at the proposed destruction of the Watch House of Plymouth and two years later represented the Society at the reopening of the Pump Rooms in Bath. Earlier, in 1931, he entertained at Swakeleys some overseas visitors, an event organized by the Victoria League of London and as we have seen also entertained the Dowager Queen Mary at a shooting party. Afterwards she sent him a signed photo which is now on display at Kiplin Hall. *(It is to be hoped that the Queen, who seems to have been something of a kleptomaniac, did not take any of Humphrey's possessions. Often a few days after her visits to country houses, embarrassed courtiers would return objects Queen Mary had taken 'by mistake').* Bridget and Humphrey were still close and she would often support him in his lobbying for the preservation of Swakeleys and other buildings, and occasionally played hostess at Swakeleys. She said of the house that 'H always said it was the best proportioned bit of architecture he knew'. He loved it so much that he had an expensive model of the house made which, after his death, Bridget offered to the SPAB.

Swakeleys is not his only memorial however. His obituary said that 'When trustee of the Ashridge Estate it was Mr Talbot's idea to bring the country branch of the Zoo to Whipsnade, when part of the estate and he negotiated the arrangement with the Zoological Society'. Millions of visitors are in his debt.

Whatever Phil Wheatley had alleged about a falling out with General Sir Reginald Talbot, H was still close to his only surviving uncle, dining with him at the General's homes at 9 York Terrace, Regent's Park and at his country home, States, by the River Thames at Medmenham in Buckinghamshire.

Reggie, still the model of a modern Major General, seems to have been greatly loved by all his family, though having no children of his own. He died on the 15th Jan, 1929 and was buried at Medmenham. He seems to have been a die-hard Protestant as his will, full of generous bequests to his relatives and friends and servants, in particular his 'butler and body servant, Archibald Fripp', contains this heartfelt plea to his wife. 'I earnestly hope she will not give or leave any property or money to Roman Catholic Institutions of any sort'. We do not know if she obeyed him but she did disobey another of his instructions, burying the General at Medmenham and not in the Talbot family graveyard in Ingestre in Staffordshire.

Humphrey was made a trustee of his uncle's estate, as he was of that of Lady Margaret, Reggie's wife. Margaret, Aunt Doobit to her nephews and nieces, was evidently a generous soul because, although wealthy, she promised more in her will than the estate would bear. When she died in 1937, H had some delicate sorting out to do, but all the Talbot children received considerable sums, jewellery and paintings as various childless relatives died. Indeed H seems to have felt uncomfortable with owning so much because, in the 1930's, he donated the Humphrey Talbot Collection to the South African National Gallery. It contains masterpieces by the Pre Raphaelite painter, Edward Burne Jones, including 'The Wood Nymph' recently 'rediscovered'.

H was almost fifty six when the Second World War began, too old to be called back to military service. He was living for much of the time in Italy, but then moved to France, escaping at the last minute, just before Dunkirk

He moved from Swakeleys, which was taken over by the Government, back to Little Gaddesden House before moving again, in 1943, to another ancient property, the Old House Clavering on the Essex/Hertfordshire border. He seemed to be living the life of an old retired bachelor. Then, at the beginning of 1944, Bridget and Kathleen received the most extraordinary news.

On January 24th The Times carried the following announcement:-

MR H.TALBOT and MRS DRUMMOND

A marriage has been arranged, and will take place at Eton College Chapel on Saturday, Feb 12th, at 2.30pm, between Humphrey Talbot....of the Old House, Clavering and formerly of Swakeleys and Mammie Drummond, widow of Captain Drummond of Berwick-on-Tweed. All friends will be welcome at the chapel.

The sisters must have been astonished, amused, delighted, and perhaps relieved. The often melancholic H could look forward to being looked after in his last years.

Who was Mammie Drummond? She was a former actress and had been in Humphrey's life for some time. She was born Mammie Whittaker and aged just sixteen, had gone on the stage. Photographs of her, taken in 1910, are in the National Portrait Gallery. She was very beautiful and appeared in the West End, but her career as an actress appears to have stalled. She had then married a Captain Drummond and now she was a widow. By 1943 she was a very important person in Humphrey's life. On the 27th March of that year, while he was in Lochgilphead in Scotland, Humphrey wrote a new will in which he left Mrs. Drummond, of 80, Cambridge St, London, an income of £250 a year. He also made her the guardian of his bequest to the Museum of South Africa in Cape Town, to be known as the 'Humphrey Talbot Collection'. She was also given a farm in Argyll and a Louis XVth table among other things. Then in January they got engaged.

But the marriage did not take place. Six days before it was due to do so, on February 6th, Humphrey was found dead in his bed in Clavering, aged sixty. It was Kathleen who notified the coroner. The cause of the death of Humphrey John Talbot, of independent means, was given as coronary thrombosis arterio-sclerosis.

His local newspaper, The Gazette, said this.

'...his marriage was going to take place at Eton College Chapel on February 12th, by special permission as a benefactor to his old school.

(He had presented some beautiful furniture to the Provosts Hall)

At the last moment the Archbishop's registrar made a technical legal mistake about the special licence and as a result Mr. Talbot decided to get married the previous Saturday at Clavering, where the banns had been asked. This entailed a lot of rearrangement and, as a result, just as he was going down to Clavering Church he had a heart attack, and the wedding did not take place. He passed peacefully away in his sleep that night.'

A memorial service was held on February 11th, at Little Gaddesden Church, at which Bridget and Kathleen and Mrs. Drummond, who was to have been married the next day, were among those present. In his will Humphrey had written 'I desire, if possible, to be cremated and my dust scattered in the wood at Swakeleys House, Uxbridge, at the East-end of the Kitchen Garden there'.....

Humphrey left an estate worth £39,753, around twelve million pounds in today's money, although the value of his paintings alone have soared well above that figure. One small bequest caught the eye of the newspapers and hinted at what Humphrey might have got up to out of the eyes of his family. He left '£25 to Edith Fowler, sometime known as the Camberwell Beauty, for a trip to Paris in memory of her florist and many jokes together'.

H's will makes fascinating reading. It reveals quite how wealthy he was, what fine works of art he possessed, and hints at a vivid social life in France.

He had two farms in Scotland and some Canadian property in British Columbia. He had so many paintings, so much jewellery, furniture and fabrics, that he could not house them all and had lent many of them to schools, clubs, museums and other great houses. He left money to his sisters and friends like Avis Spurway, nee Hodgson and Ruth Blezzard, as well as to Eton, to libraries, to museums, to Governments, to the Society for the Protection of Ancient Buildings, and of course to the Humphrey Talbot collection in South Africa. Also included in that collection are all Humphrey's 'Toys ...Cart and Horse, Lighthouse, Bathing Machine etc'.

Apart from the 'Camberwell Beauty' a number of other ladies received jewellery and paintings, including two who lived near Bayonne in France. Another gift to France gives a clue to where they might have met Humphrey and why he was grateful to them. He left a Burne Jones painting, 'Love disguised as Reason', to the Bonnat Gallery, Bayonne. H asked that an inscription be added to it. 'In memory of Happy Days at Brindos and Bayonne - Don de H.J.Talbot.'

The Chateau de Brindos, near Bayonne, is now owned by the former French rugby star, Serge Blanco. It claims that it is still decorated in the unmistakable style of the Roaring Twenties when its cocktails were world famous. In the thirties it was taken over by the entrepreneur, art enthusiast and traveller, Sir Reginald Wright. The Chateau's brochure says that guests 'danced to the music of Cole Porter and beautiful women in Chanel lay on the sundrenched terraces, taking advantage of the evening light so particular to the Basque country. The lake lent itself to all kinds of extravagances'. No wonder H was happy there and perhaps dreamed of returning with Mammie when the war was over. Now he had 'returned to dust' and there were only two Talbots of Little Gaddesden left alive.

Kathleen

Kathleen was fifty when her second brother died. She continued with her work for the Village Produce Associations and when the war ended, also resumed her musical career with Dorothy. She became involved in the Rural Schools Movement and according to

Barbara Cassell, from this she realised two things; first, 'the need for County Music Advisers with attendant local support - the growth of some excellent Youth Orchestras stems from this and secondly, that there should be some training available for amateur conductors of choirs and orchestras'. She helped start the Talbot Lampton Music School.

Dorothy Erhart, meanwhile, was still giving concerts and teaching music in London. In 1952 names appear once again in the K's visitors' book and many were from Nigeria, some from the British Council.

Once more musical evenings took place at The Manor House, including piano recitals by Anthony Hopkins who lived nearby. There were Elizabethan Serenades and other events, all at a modest price and sometimes with a glass of wine included. Then in 1958 K's sister Bridget was knocked down on a pedestrian crossing in London and laid up in a nursing home with a broken leg. As B was now almost seventy three and few Talbots seemed to live into a ripe old age, Kathleen was worried for her health and hurried to the home, only to find B in full flow, ordering the staff about and driving them to distraction.

However it was the younger sister who was to die first.

Kathleen and Dorothy often travelled to Salzburg, once home to Mozart, for the musical festivals. It was there on the 2nd of July, 1958 that K died suddenly of a heart attack, the old Talbot weakness that had killed her father at sixty five and Humphrey at the age of sixty. She was sixty four and because of her private, modest, nature, it is possible few even of her family knew quite how much she had achieved. The obituaries in The Times reveal the shock felt by friends and the love and admiration they held for her. Dr Reginald Jacques wrote:-

It was in connection with the organization of County Music Festivals and the Rural Conductors' School (which was founded by her and will be celebrating its 21st anniversary this year) that Kathleen was most widely known. She had a genius for making and keeping friends and stimulating one of the most valuable elements of our national life, the constant collaboration of professional and amateur musicians.

She gave herself unsparingly to this work, and her influence will never die.

This would seem a sufficiently fulsome tribute, but a few days later Mrs. D. Fitzherbert added the following, under the headline 'Augmenting the National Larder':-

'In your obituary notice it is surprising to find no mention of Miss Talbot's work in the Second World War for which she was appointed an MBE.

She quickly realized what a large and valuable addition for the national larder could be made by village gardens. Having persuaded the authorities of this she became founder and honorary organizer of the Village Produce Association movement and devoted most of her energy to this from 1939 to her death. The idea caught on quickly and by the end of the war covered virtually the whole of England and Wales. Many will remember how KT travelled all over the country – under all the discomforts and difficulties of wartime transport – to persuade people of the importance of domestic food production.

Her wonderful gift for getting on with country people was invaluable in this work and her ability to persuade them to co-operate did much to improve diet in those lean years. It was a bitter blow when, after the war, official backing was withdrawn from the VPAs but, undaunted, she set to work to rebuild the shattered movement. It is largely due to her courage and vision that the National Federation of VPAs is now firmly established as an independent voluntary organization and is steadily growing. She was very pleased indeed that, shortly before her death, it was officially recognized again.

She will live on in the hearts of her friends all over the country, in all walks of life and many who did not know her will have reason to thank her for the friendly atmosphere of their local VPA.

Countrywoman born and bred, she had thorough knowledge of gardening and the use of garden produce that was the hallmark in the older days of the good housewife.

In addition she was a most notable cook.'

Still her friends thought there was more to say.

On the 18th July 1958 Viscountess Davidson (the wife of Bridget's arch enemy) wrote:-

The tragically sudden death of Miss Kathleen Talbot has come as a great shock to her multitude of friends and admirers. To those like myself who were associated with her in some of her many interests the sense of loss is profound indeed. She inspired affections by her enthusiasm and perseverance in every thing she did. She represented all that was best in village life. She typified the best of the old world combined with an imaginative understanding of this new and ever changing world. She will be mourned and long remembered by everyone who was privileged to know her.

A memorial service was held on July 19th in Little Gaddesden church. Both Bridget and Dorothy were present. K's body was cremated, like Humphrey's and her ashes laid underneath a cherry tree next to the grave of her brother Geoffrey and their parents. Her will reveals that Kathleen had at least six godchildren, including Avis *(Hodgson)* Spurway's daughter Mary.

In her will she left the Manor House to Dorothy *(whose surname is spelt with a 'd' in the document)*. She and K's cousin, the artist Roger De Grey, were made trustees and after Dorothy's death, de Grey and Avis were to inherit the estate. When Dorothy herself died in 1971 her ashes were also placed under the cherry tree.

Bridget

Bridget Elizabeth Talbot was now seventy three years old and the last surviving Talbot of Little Gaddesden. She had hoped to have a role on the national stage, in Westminster politics, but that had come to nothing. National Labour, which she had joined in 1931, had withered away.

Judging by a poem she wrote, apparently published locally in 1949, but we suspect composed earlier, she now favoured the party of Clement Attlee and Ernie Bevin.

191

Part of the poem reads:-

The Tory's policy, they say,
Is let the money make its way.
Destroy the country fair and bright:
The speculator must be right.
The richest folk must have their choice,
The worker must not lift his voice,
However much he needs a House"...

It ends:-

Farewell, farewell to village dear
With cherry trees on Green so fair.
Now strive with all your main and might
For LABOUR and get things put right.

However B was no Socialist, and nothing could have persuaded her to join the hated Conservatives, so she became a Liberal and stood as the party's candidate in Bermondsey and Rotherhithe, one of the poorest parts of London in the election in February 1950.

Her campaign literature proclaimed that 'You can have a LIBERAL GOVERNMENT this time', but she must have known it was a 'no hope' seat and she was duly slaughtered at the polls.

The winner was an old school class warrior, Labour's Bob Mellish, later a particularly tough Chief Whip under Harold Wilson. He polled 26,018 votes. The Conservative was second, with 5,964.

Miss Bridget Talbot, Liberal, won just 1,852 votes.

It was the end of her political career, though in 1964, aged seventy nine, she considered standing for Richmond in the General Election, in opposition to the Common Market.

In 1961 she privately published a book, 'Sea Saga', in which she bewailed the fact that she could not have done more for her country, or rather that her country had not listened to her more. She also renewed he attack on the Davidsons:-

'At one particular pre-war local political meeting our MP Mrs. Davidson spoke. Her husband had just returned from the distressed areas where he had been sent to report on what could be done for the two million unemployed. There is nothing much we can do, he had said – a welfare club here or there. Unaccustomed to public speaking, I leapt to my feet, horrified at such an irresponsible answer. I demanded to know why with the growing menace of Germany we could not build ships and aeroplanes and keep our men from the miserable existence of the dole and the means test –Why not clear slums and build? It could have been done then at a fraction of what it cost after the war, and money was not inflated. At subsequent meetings I brought up the subject of our declining sea power again and again. Viscountess Davidson (as she had now become) told me from the platform that I had a bee in my bonnet about our shipping. My reply was that it was a bee I was very proud to have in my bonnet, because on our shipping we depended for half our food and our very existence. I returned to the attack over and over again, but with no success.'

She wrote in despair, 'For 30 years I have struggled hopelessly to awake this country to the danger of losing our sea power. It is disastrous to see our Merchant Navy and our Royal Navy dwindling and fading away'.

She turned her attention back to her charitable work. As well as continuing to support the Watch Ashore, she was appointed Vice President of the Red Ensign Club. She also became an Honorary Committee Member of St Dunstan's Training for the Blind and continued to have members to tea at Little Gaddesden House and was active in the Summer Camps.

Her childhood home was now far too big for her and she let out various parts in an attempt to raise enough money to avoid selling it. Despite various legacies she appears to have been what we would now call 'cash poor' yet she now owned an even bigger house as well, at Scorton, near Northallerton, in North Yorkshire. Bridget had loved Kiplin Hall since childhood and there are many photographs of her and her brothers and sister holidaying there, riding in the grounds or boating on the small lake.

There was a double family connection. One of Alfred Talbot's elder brothers, Walter, had married Beatrice de Grey, the sister of Alfred's wife, so their children were cousins twice over.

Walter Talbot had inherited Kiplin from a great uncle in 1868, but there were conditions attached. He must marry a Protestant and remain one himself and every seven years his faith had to be tested by a team of Anglican clergymen. He of course complied. He also had to change his name; so Walter Talbot became Captain, later Admiral, Walter Carpenter of Kiplin Hall.

The House had been built in the early 1620's by a local gentleman, George Calvert, who was born close by. Calvert was secretary to James 1st. He became the 1st Lord Baltimore in 1625 and founded Maryland, in what is now the USA, in 1632. The building's elegant design in fashionable red brick was unusual in Jacobean architecture, with domed towers on the centre of each side of a tall symmetrical structure.

Until the Admiral's death in 1904 (another Talbot heart attack) the Carpenter family enjoyed the typical country house lifestyle of the period with house parties, shooting, fishing, boating, tennis, theatricals and music, and the Talbot family of Little Gaddesden enjoyed it with them.

The Admiral left most of the estate to his daughter, Sarah, who three years later married and moved to Lincolnshire. The Hall was rented to tenants, there was very little income and it fell into decline.

By 1938 Sarah had sold off much of the buildings and land and the estate was reduced from over five thousand acres to the house and one hundred and twenty acres of gardens.

She then made Bridget, who was nine years younger, joint owner of Kiplin, as B was already sharing the struggle to find a use for the property. When Sarah died in 1957 it became B's sole responsibility, and it was a heavy one.

To quote the Kiplin Hall guidebook :-

'Miss Talbot's struggle to save Kiplin lasted for more than 40 years.... She advertised it as a conference centre in the 1930's and as a guest house for visitors from America and the Dominions in the 1950's...

In 1953, she wrote a pageant called 'Farewell Kiplin', to be performed by local people and local and national newspapers carried the story of the imminent demolition of the Hall.

Her great hope was the National Trust, but they refused to take Kiplin on, and in April 1958 an article in The Times carried the headline Yorkshire Mansion to be Demolished'.

Did Bridget really contemplate demolition or was she imposing artificial deadlines in an increasingly desperate attempt to find a future for her inheritance?

According to the Kiplin guidebook, that London traffic accident came to the rescue because, as Bridget was in a London nursing home with a broken leg, she did not telephone the demolition firm and the Hall remained standing.

Finally Bridget had a brainwave. She set up the Kiplin Hall Trust and registered it with the Charity Commission in February 1968. Its purpose was 'To hold Kiplin Hall and its appurtenances upon Trust permanently to preserve the same for the benefit of the nation as a place of beauty and historical and architectural interest'. Her cousin, Hugh Chetwynd Talbot, was the first Chairman of Trustees and when Bridget died she left the contents of the house to the Trustees in her will. However it was still largely derelict.

Yet Kiplin Hall survives today, over forty years later, can be visited and has never looked finer. It is full of paintings and photographs of the Talbots and in a room at the top of the house, just off the Long Gallery, is a room devoted to Bridget and her siblings. It is a wonderful memorial to her.

That the House is now in such good condition is due partly to the State of Maryland, which repaired the roof, and partly to a difficult but courageous decision by the Trustees to sacrifice part of the historic parkland for the extraction of gravel in the 1990's. It gave the estate a genuine chance of long term survival. To the first time visitor in 2012, who had not seen what was lost, the resulting lake simply added to the appeal of the view from the dining room windows. The Countryside Commission had also helped the Trustees to buy back thirty acres of parkland sold in 1930.

So Bridget Talbot 'saved' Kiplin Hall, just as she 'saved' Ashridge Park. Her childhood home in Little Gaddesden was saved as well, though it did not become the charitable home she hoped it would be. Instead it was divided into several properties and some of her letters put on a skip during the building work. Fortunately many of those letters found their way to Kiplin Hall.

In her last years Bridget became even more of a 'character'. Tales of her eccentricity are legendary in Little Gaddesden – some stories no doubt artfully honed over the years but generally told with exasperated amusement:- how she used to regularly paint her old car a different colour or better still get the Scouts to do it for her; how she would leave said car in the middle of the road causing an obstruction in Little Gaddesden or, in Berkhamsted, stop in the middle of the High Street by the shops, bank, or police station, toot the horn and expect the lower orders to come and serve her there and then, despite the angry traffic jam building up behind her; how she would buy a couple of tiny paint pots from the hardware store in the village and command that they be carried to her car; how, being short of a hat for a formal occasion she turned up wearing a decorated plant pot; how, when aiming to slow down the traffic in Little Gaddesden, she found a mannequin dummy, dressed it, took out her paints again and painted it blood red and threw it into the road as a warning to those speeding residents who didn't comply with her stop speeding signs she'd also painted on the road; how she never cared about her appearance wearing the clothes, according to one account, of 'a lady of the road'; how she stopped regularly to relieve her bladder in the bushes of a particular lay-by on the only 5 mile car drive to Berkhamsted; how she acquired- somehow-hairs from the manes of the Queen's greys at Westminster during the Coronation of 1953.

Kerry Hardie remembered being taken to see Bridget and wanting to go 'because she had the most wonderful old chair which was really a musical box that played when you sat on it.... My mother still remembered what Bridget said to her when she was told we were going back to Ireland:
'But my dear, you can't do that, nobody lives in Ireland any more.'
The former pupils of Little Gaddesden Junior School remembered Maypole dancing outside The Manor House and the subsequent parties in the village hall.
'I especially remember the formidable presence of 'Miss Talbot', who lurched dangerously around in an ancient car.... and used to throw sweets to us throngs of children in the village hall. Once I remember her throwing us buns in the car park!
Another remembered being May Queen and 'riding on Bridget Talbot's pony, Cherry'. On what Bridget decided was Mayday (it could be anywhere between April and June) a cousin, Humphrey Chetwynd-Talbot, would be summoned to help with B's celebrations. First the children would be separated off and sent to the stables where they would be given cakes and lemonade. The adults would be taken into Little Gaddesden House which was by now very run down. Humphrey Talbot remembers torn curtains, threadbare carpets and lots of dry rot. The place was falling apart, but B seemed not to notice. Then everyone assembled outside and the children were made to hold onto a rope and follow the donkey to a Maypole put up outside The Manor House. A small band of blind musicians from St Dunstan's marched alongside the strange procession.

Humphrey says that Bridget often swam in a very cold outdoor swimming pool. He was told to pull the curtains and not to look as B's swimming costume was full of holes.
Barbara Cassell, another relative, thought B had something of the naughty schoolgirl about her and said she was always encouraging children to be slightly naughty.

She was not 'reliable' and enjoyed being 'a character....There were many tales of quite grand people being invited to lunch or tea, who arrived to find no Bridget and no food'.

Then there were the occasions when she travelled on the train without a ticket, and she was twice prosecuted for this.

Dorothy Erhart had a lovely story of going to Euston (with B) when both had rail tickets; however, when she was asked for a ticket at Euston, she flatly refused to find one- so the inspector was called. After all the fuss was over Dorothy asked her 'Why did you make this fuss when I saw you buy a ticket?' Bridget's answer was that it was in her raincoat pocket, but underneath some extremely useful lavatory paper labelled 'British Rail' and she was not 'going to turn her pocket out in front of an inspector'.

She was a rebel to the end. Aristocratic eccentrics like Bridget are a great rarity these days – and perhaps, in some ways, the world is less colourful without them.

Bridget Elizabeth Talbot died at Kiplin on the 29th November 1971, the last of the Talbots of Little Gaddesden. She was eighty six years old. There was a private service at Kiplin Hall on Dec 3rd. 'No flowers by request'. Born before the age of the motor car, she had lived to see man land on the moon.

Bridget rewrote her will three weeks before she died and in it she remembered Avis (Hodgson) Spurway, K's wartime nursing companion and one of the few of her cousins and friends still living. She was most concerned that her servants and housekeepers, like Mrs.Macadam at Little Gaddesden, should be able to continue to live on in her houses and cottages. Trustees had been appointed for both of her main properties. 'It is my earnest hope', she wrote 'that so far as possible the Little Gaddesden House Trustees may be able to provide a real home for children between the ages of five and ten years or as a convalescent home for children and adults preferably the orphans of fathers who have been in the Royal Navy or the Merchant Marine and that by letting off some of the rooms to produce rents and by means of grants the property may become self supporting'.

Unfortunately this does not seem to have been possible as Bridget had not organized her tax affairs carefully and had died when tax rates were particularly high. Her estate was considerable, it was valued at £256,6337 net, but the duty paid was £152,745.

B had one final request. 'I wish my body to be cremated and that my ashes be scattered over the little stream off the grass road between Edlesborough and Ivinghoe in view of the nine miles stretch of wood and country and I would like a stone put up on the bridge near the stream and another on Ivinghoe Down to say that I saved them for the National Trust. I hope that later a small memorial service may be held in the Kiplin Hall Chapel and one in the Chapel of the Red Ensign Club the latter with reference to the red torch which I invented and which saved hundreds of sailors' lives during the war'. The memorial services were indeed held as she wished.

Epilogue – A Talbot Trail

There are no Talbots left in Little Gaddesden, but much of what they, their family and friends, saw and loved, we can see too, thanks in no small part to the work of Bridget and Humphrey and Kathleen.

One autumn afternoon, when the beech woods of the Chilterns were in all their golden glory we set out on a Talbot trail.

We began in the old town of Hemel Hempstead, untouched by the post war new town development, where it would be no surprise to see a member of the family in a horse pulled 'fly' coming down the high street to shop. The eighteenth century pubs and houses and the nineteenth century old town hall look a little like a film set and have been used as one.

We took the now quiet road north passed Gade Park for half a mile before we reached the hamlet of Piccotts End, where Conty Sitwell the diarist and her father, the local MP, Gustavus Adolphus Talbot, lived.

Their house, Marchmont, is now a pub restaurant, the Marchmont Arms, tastefully restored but otherwise little altered. The River Gade flows gently through the water meadows below and horses graze in the fields beyond.

Cars on the by-pass can be heard, but not seen, behind a screen of trees. Almost opposite, a large Roman villa was discovered with extensive hot water baths, the remains now buried once more. The Gaddesden Valley has been a pleasant place to live for millennia.

(Conty did not return to live here after her husband, General Sitwell, died at the Northumbrian family home in Barmoor in 1932. Instead she moved to Victoria Square in London, near Buckingham Palace, where she could see her London friends, write her books and pursue her fascination with spiritualism. She became President of the College of Psychic Science and died, aged eighty seven, in 1974.)

Going North through Piccotts End, we passed on our right the row of cottages, once a medieval infirmary, where some remarkable fifteenth century wall paintings have been found. They

would have delighted Humphrey. We then turned right onto the Leighton Buzzard road and after passing the nineteenth century Red Lion, turned left immediately before the old bridge at Water End, where watercress beds were harvested, and headed for the hamlet of Nettleden, on the edge of Ashridge Park. It is even smaller than it was a hundred years ago, but Nettleden House, where the Talbot's cousin, the artist Cooie Lane, lived with her widowed mother until 1936, is still there, opposite the tiny church of St Laurence. *(After her mother's death Cooie moved up the hill to a cottage in St Margarets, near a medieval nunnery, where she died in 1944. It was here that she wrote her book 'The Three Rectories', published by her niece Barbara Cassell, nee Lane, in 2004. There is now a Buddhist monastery nearby.*
With her friend, the artist Dora Carrington, Cooie painted three frescoes at Ashridge House which are still there).
The old medieval road to Little Gaddesden once continued past Nettleden and along the bottom of the Golden Valley to Witchcraft Bottom, but at the beginning of the 19th century the Bridgewaters, who then owned Ashridge, expanded the park, closed that road off and created a new road which turns right and climbs to the top of the hill.

A mile and a half after leaving Nettleden, the outskirts of Little Gaddesden appeared. Although Bridget's arch enemy, J.C.C.Davidson, Chairman of the Conservative party, did build some new houses on the left hand side of the road, there is little twentieth century building elsewhere, and most of the houses would have been known to the Talbots. Their childhood home, Little Gaddesden House, is still there at the top of the ridge, with wonderful views East and West. Bridget's fears that it would be pulled down have proved unfounded. The house is now occupied by several families, but little has changed on the outside, though there is no longer a painted policeman at the entrance to the drive or a formidable old lady at the end of it.
A few hundred yards further on, just past the road to Hudnall, is Kathleen's post war home, The Manor House, to which she moved in 1924. When the Talbot children were growing up it

was occupied by Colonel and Mrs.Wheatley and their three girls, one of whom, Angel, was a good friend of K from childhood. Pearl Wheatley, her sister, lived until 1985 and kept in contact with the Ashridge archivist until the end and helped with the writing of the history of the estate.

The Manor House and surrounding buildings are now lived in by five families. If you knock on the front door of that part which is now called The Manor House and, if they are in, Roger and Julia Bolton will be glad to show you where Kathleen and Dorothy Erhart gave their recitals beneath the painting of the arrest of Queen, then Princess, Elizabeth and they will gladly give you a cup of tea!

Next to The Manor House, but a little further up the green, is the memorial Lord Brownlow had erected to his beloved wife Adelaide, who died in 1917. If you stand in front of it you can see the entrance to Ashridge House some way below you, a vista having been cut through the beech trees. It enabled Adelbert, the Earl, to see the monument every morning when in residence.

From that Ashridge House entrance another, longer, vista leads to the Bridgewater Monument, a memorial to the 'Father of Inland Navigation'. Next to the monument is a National Trust shop and outside it a number of medallions which celebrate those who helped to preserve the estate. Bridget Talbot's name is on one of them.

Back in Little Gaddesden we travelled North-West along the Green, to possibly the oldest building in the village, John O'Gaddesden's House. In front of it is a war memorial, designed by Mrs.Wheatley, with Geoffrey's name upon it.

Every Remembrance Day there is a memorial service there where all twenty four villagers who died in the two World Wars are remembered.

At the dedication of this memorial, in 1921, the service sheet displayed the following three quotations:-

'Live thou for England — we for England died.
Yesterday returneth not, perchance tomorrow cometh not.
This is thine hour — misuse it not.'

A few yards further on, we turned into Church Road, passing the village hall, originally a nissen hut erected during the Second World War. There the Village Produce Association, which Kathleen founded, still flourishes, as does the Drama Club, though plays and pantomimes, not masques, are now produced there. The Boy Scouts, started by Bridget, still have a hut behind the Hall, but Geoffrey's brass band is no more. Perhaps, like us, he spent lazy summer afternoons watching cricket being played in the field opposite, or wielded a bat himself.

We carried on down the road and soon the houses gave way to open countryside and there, isolated on the hill overlooking the Gade valley, is Little Gaddesden church. Disturbances in the surrounding fields suggest the original village was next to the church until the catastrophe of the Black Death, when it moved closer to Ashridge monastery.

Many Talbots, including Alfred and his wife, are buried there. Geoffrey has two memorials. One is a stone strip across his parents' grave, to the north-east of the nave. The other, close by, the standard white military headstone, with name, rank and date of death.

But the names of Humphrey, Bridget and Katheen are not to be seen. It is believed that K's ashes were sprinkled by a cherry blossom tree which adjoined her parents' grave, and that Dorothy Erhart's ashes followed later, but of the tree there is now no sign. For some reason there is also no headstone to either of the friends. It is also thought that Humphrey's ashes were scattered, as he requested, some miles away at Swakeleys, near Uxbridge. There is no stone here to him either. And Bridget? There is a memorial but it is not here.

We got back into the car, drove back along Church Road, turned right and headed for Dagnall and the Leighton Buzzard road. Two miles north-west of Dagnall, no more than three miles from Little Gaddesden, is the medieval Edlesborough church, now redundant, but full of the most remarkable wooden carvings. It stands on what may be a man-made mound giving superb views over the Vale of Aylesbury.

Bridget sometimes attended services there. As Barbara Cassell said, 'Which church Bridget Talbot worshipped at depended on which vicar she was currently agreeing with. When we stayed with her we slept in her Italian bed, which had a magnificent head-piece but no foot-piece. She told us the missing piece was behind the altar in Edlesborough church to brighten it up'.

By the side of the church a path leads south-west to Ivinghoe. We walked along it in the late autumn sunshine. To our left the Chiltern Hills rose up to Ivinghoe Beacon, site of a prehistoric fort. Halfway down lay the equally old Icknield Way which innumerable invaders had followed South to Salisbury plain.

Romans, Anglo Saxons, Vikings and Normans had all used it and it became a sort of medieval motorway filled with travellers heading north-east to Dunstable and the King's Palace and the Priory there. Just below the Way and the modern road, is the waterline from where streams flow down and eventually feed into the Great Ouse, heading for Bedford and then into the North Sea, where Bridget sailed on the four-masted sailing ship the Pamir in 1937.

Crossing the little Whistle Brook, where it emerges from Coombe Bottom, we saw a horizontal stone bench on the far side.

On it is carved these words.

IN MEMORY OF
BRIDGET ELIZABETH TALBOT O.B.E.
Of Little Gaddesden and Kiplin Hall
SEAMAN'S FRIEND AND DEFENDER OF HUMAN RIGHTS.
She helped preserve these Downs for you who read this.
Died 29th Nov. 1971
Inventor of life saving water tight torch for mariners.

Bridget Elizabeth Talbot was not one to hide her light under a bushel – but there was a lot of light.

We sat down on the bench as the sun slipped down to the horizon and twilight began, lifted our eyes to the hills and thought of Bridget and Humphrey and Geoffrey and Kathleen, the last Talbots of Little Gaddesden.

Acknowledgements

This book exists only because Andrew Graham-Stewart kept the letters left in The Manor House and because Dawn Webster of Kiplin Hall let us have others and also sent us extracts from Bridget's diaries. Dawn answered innumerable questions with an ever present smile and made us most welcome at Kiplin, a beautiful house which anyone interested in the Talbots should visit. They are the 'onlie begetters' of this history.

In Little Gaddesden, the late Barbara Cassell shared memories of her Talbot friends and relatives and we are also very grateful to the many villagers who passed on stories about Bridget, who, over forty years after her death, is vividly remembered.

At Ashridge House, the archivist and head gardener, Mick Thompson, gave us copies of Bridget's rather subjective account of the sale and other documents. We hope he writes his own book about Ashridge one day.

Our thanks also go to the Society for the Preservation of Ancient Buildings which gave us the run of the library in their exquisite seventeenth century home near Spitalfields in London and to the security guard at Swakeleys who showed us around the building when we turned up unannounced.

Finally, we would like to celebrate the glory that is the British Library. Together with the internet it provides an entry into a past we so nearly lost.

Authors' Notes

ROGER AND JULIA BOLTON both worked in broadcasting. Julia made documentaries and worked as a news producer for nearly twenty years before retraining to become a teacher. Roger was a BBC executive and then ran his own independent production company. He now presents Feedback for BBC Radio 4. They have lived in Little Gaddesden for over twenty years and own The Manor House which once belonged to Kathleen Talbot.

Lightning Source UK Ltd.
Milton Keynes UK
UKOW05f0347241013

219648UK00001B/10/P